JEWISH CHRISTIANITY
H. E. DANA

Jewish Christianity

An Expository Survey of Acts I to XII,
James, I and II Peter, Jude and Hebrews

•

H. E. DANA

*Professor of New Testament Interpretation
in the Southwestern Baptist
Theological Seminary*

•

WIPF & STOCK · Eugene, Oregon

Wipf and Stock Publishers
199 W 8th Ave, Suite 3
Eugene, OR 97401

Jewish Christianity
An Expository Survey of Acts i to Xii,
James, I and II, Jude and Hebrews
By Dana, H.E.
ISBN 13: 978-1-5326-1319-7
Publication date 10/24/2016
Previously published by
Bible Institute Memorial Press, 1937

Reverently Dedicated

To the Memory of

B. H. CARROLL

Saint-Scholar-Prophet

PREFACE

Jewish Christianity of the first century has been a neglected subject. It is remarkable how little distinctive treatment has been given to this phase of development in primitive Christianity. It has generally been regarded as but a sort of prelude to the establishment of Christianity in the Gentile world. Doubtless this attitude has been created by the relatively brief account which Luke gives in the first twelve chapters of Acts, where Jewish Christianity appears as a sort of approach to the missionary activities of Paul. The popular conception has been that the entire history of Palestinian Christianity for the first fifty years of its development was contained in these opening chapters of Acts. This, however, is a wholly inadequate view. A little reflection and comparison of evidences convinces one that Luke has selected but a single thread in the vast texture of a great historical period.

We have in this period of early Christian history a distinct and foundational development. It is here that the streams arose which have swept out in the vast tides of world evangelization. It was in these momentous days of beginning that the evangelic tradition was formulated which appears in our Gospels, and the redemptive message originated which is the great theme of the epistles and of Christian teaching in all the subsequent ages.

In the treatment of this period there has been a vast modification of viewpoint in the past century. This progressive alteration in point of view may be seen in four books belonging entirely or in part to this field of study. The first is by Cartwright, *The Hebrew Christian Church of Jerusalem* (London, 1842), which views Jerusalem Christianity as presenting the totality of primitive Jewish Christian development, and as having advanced along conscious and purposeful ecclesiastical lines. The author viewed all Palestinian Christianity as of one piece, centering in and largely embraced by the Jerusalem church. This represents the prevailing conception for seventy-five years. At the beginning of the present century the understanding of this period began to be altered, but that the change was very slow may be seen in *The Earliest Christian Church* (Cambridge, 1929) by Hunkin, a really scholarly work, but one that sees Jewish Christianity only in the early chapters of Acts. A radical departure, pressing far toward the other extreme of ignoring Acts entirely, may be found in Kundsin, "Primitive Christianity In the Light of Gospel Research", a translation published by F. C. Grant in his *Form Criticism* (Chicago, 1934). A more conservative view, though still maintaining a large degree of independence from Acts, is represented in Riddle, *Early Christian Life* (Chicago, 1936). As scholars work toward a position between these two extremes, utilizing inferences from the Gospel material and giving careful consideration at the same time to Acts, we will begin to secure a new and highly profitable insight into the large history of this vital phase of primitive Christian life. The present work undertakes a contributioin to this line of investigation from the conservative viewpoint.

There is necessarily much of the speculative in the discussion of Palestinian Christianity. Luke devotes his record primarily to the Jerusalem church, and beyond that we are dependent on reasonable probability and inferences from the points of interest reflected in the Gospels, chiefly the Synoptics. But an assembly of all the evidence presents a gratifying enlargement of our knowledge of distinctive Jewish Christianity.

The English text of the New Testament has not been printed with this commentary. It is designed to be studied with the New Testament open before the student, beside the commentary. This is quite important, for it is the only effective way in which this commentary may be used. In many places the author gives his own translation of the Greek text, but in these translations there is a large element of paraphrase, so the student should have his English text open before him that he may there follow the more literal sense.

The author is indebted to Messrs. Herbert J. Miles and A. T. Pilgreen for assistance in research, and to his wife and Mr. Carl A. Clark for the preparation of the manuscript for publication.

H. E. DANA,

Seminary Hill, Texas

CONTENTS

CHAPTER	PAGE
I. Introduction	13

PART ONE. PALESTINIAN JEWISH CHRISTIANITY.

II. The Galilean Disciples	27
III. The Judean Disciples	36
IV. The Message of Palestinian Christianity	59

PART TWO. HELLENISTIC JEWISH CHRISTIANITY.

V. Christianity and the Synagogue—The Epistle of James	97
VI. Christianity and the Dispersion—The Epistles of Peter and Jude	128
VII. The Widening Breach Between Christianity and Judaism—Epistle to the Hebrews	197

ADDENDUM—

Reactionary Jewish Christianity	273
Literature	279

Chapter I

INTRODUCTION

For fifteen years or more after the Ascension Christianity presented the aspect of a modified form of Judaism. It was a new manifestation of age-old and essential elements in Jewish life: those elements which pertained to the Messiah and the promised deliverance of Israel. There was no consciousness on the part of those first Jewish disciples who preached the Resurrection of Jesus that they represented a distinct religious movement. In their own minds they were still adherents of Judaism—indeed, they regarded themselves as more truly Israelites than their countrymen who had rejected the Messiah. Rather than proposing to forsake Judaism, they sought to bring it to perfect fruition of its hope and destiny. They believed themselves to be the real recipients and exponents of the heritage of Abraham. It would perhaps be more accurate to define the life and thought of these earliest disciples as Christian Judaism than Jewish Christianity.

DOCUMENTARY SOURCES

There are two literary sources from which we may derive knowledge of early Christian life. Our earliest direct source is the book of Acts—particularly the first twelve chapters. Through the generations of the past it has been regarded as axiomatic that these early chapters of Acts were our only source of knowledge relative to early Palestinian Christianity, but in the present century scholars are coming more and more to recognize another primitive and important source. The churches of Palestine are looking out at us between every line of our Synoptic Gospels. The evidence from this source is inferential, and to a considerable extent speculative, for which reason it must be thoroughly sifted and rigidly tested, but it is evidence which we cannot wisely overlook.

We know that Jesus spoke volumes of teaching which was never recorded. It would take a fair sized library to hold all he taught, while we have only a few score pages of his teaching. The varied events of the crowded years of his public ministry would fill yet other volumes. Only a small fragment of his teaching and a few events of his life were preserved in Palestinian tradition and recorded in the Gospels. What determined the selection of the material which was preserved and recorded? Three theories are possible in solution of this problem.

(1) One might suppose that the materials of our Synoptic Gospels were gathered by mere chance—a sort of grab-bag method. But convincingly refuting such a theory is the evident earnestness and seriousness of a sincere practical purpose. While the Gospels as a whole do not present any effort at careful analy-

tical organization, there are general themes and common principals running throughout. The materials of these great documents could not have been snatched up at random.

(2) One might suppose an arbitrary divine selection of the materials presented in our Gospels. To the question, why were just these materials selected, some would reply that the Holy Spirit, by His own independent and supernatural processes, directed the inspired writers to record just the accounts of life and teaching which according to His inscrutable purpose should be preserved for us. Against this theory stands the self-evident principle of divine revelation. God has revealed Himself through real, normal processes of experience, and not by arbitrary manipulation of human agency. When God uses human agency He allows it to remain human, and does not deprive it of its essential character because divinely employed. There are great basal reasons of real life lying behind the material of our Synoptic Gospels.

(3) In those Gospels there are materials which were preserved, perpetuated, and crystalized into a common tradition by the first century Palestinian churches. These traditions arose in response to the needs and exigencies which existed in the life of the churches. Consequently, we can discern facts about the life and thought of the first century Palestinian churches by searching diligently for the reasons why they preserved just the traditions which they did relative to their divine Master.

This of course does not mean that they *invented* the tradition which they desired, but that they *adapted* the authentic traditions of the life and teaching of Jesus to the needs which confronted them. There were conditions which demanded relief, errors to be corrected, convictions to be reinforced, objections to be met, arguments to be refuted, distresses to be mitigated, and many other definite developments in the experience of the disciples and the life of the churches for which the teaching and example of the Master were needed. These developments may be discerned by reconstructing the evident background of the Gospel narratives. In this way much can be learned about the life in the early Jewish churches which otherwise could only be vaguely supposed, if detected at all.

However, it still remains and must ever remain a fact that the best and most definite source of light upon this important period is to be found in the first to the twelfth chapters of Acts. The book of Acts was written by Luke, the companion of Paul, author of the third Gospel. The question of its date is unsettled, but we may be sure it was composed within the quarter century between 60 and 85 A. D. The overwhelming weight of scholarly opinion would place the writing of the book in the later years of that period, but there are strong arguments for an early date—60 to 65.

Acts is usually thought of as a book of history, but it was primarily designed as a message of teaching. Only a small portion of the actual text is devoted

JEWISH CHRISTIANITY 17

to discourse material, but the narrative material was primarily didactic in the purose of the author. His design was to describe the advancement of the Christian message from its home in Jerusalem to the center of the Roman world. He states the scope and purpose of his book in 1:8, "But ye shall receive power by the enduement of the Holy Spirit upon you, and ye shall be my witnesses, first in Jerusalem, then in all Judea and Samaria, and then on to the limit of the earth." It is the Spirit-inspired testimony of those who witnessed for Christ of which Luke desires to tell.

The plan of the narrative is indicated. The outline of Acts as it appeared to the mind of Luke might be adapted to modern forms of analysis as follows: part one, witnessing in Jerusalem; part two, witnessing in the country about Jerusalem; part three, witnessing in the lands beyond. The idiom of the Greek makes this mode of division clearer than does our ordinary English versions. The first part includes what we now know as chapters 1 to 7; the second, chapters 8 to 12; the third, chapters 13 to 28. It was in part three that Luke was predominantly interested, for there he told of the activities of his teacher and hero, the Apostle Paul.

Our interest here is in only parts one and two of Luke's record, where he throws important light on the development of Palestinian Christianity and its eventual extension to Hellenistic Judaism. Hence we shall not follow Luke's historical outline, nor treat the book in the consecutive order of its chapters, but interpret the material of the first twelve chapters in connection with the development of Jewish Christian life.

JEWISH CHRISTIANITY AND THE TEMPLE

The first rallying point of Jewish Christianity was the courts of the holy Temple. Subsequently we shall see evidences that there were many communities of disciples outside Jerusalem, even in far away Galilee, but they looked toward Jerusalem as the rightful center of their activities, and the place at which the returning Messiah would establish his final reign upon the earth.

This was a most natural attitude. To the Jew the chief symbol of Jehovah's presence, and the one place of proper approach to Him, was the Temple in Jerusalem. This conception had been instilled into Jewish Christians from earliest childhood. Hence it is not surprising that it was not immediately abandoned.

In the Lucan writings, especially Acts, is where this centrality of the Temple in Palestinian Christianity is most specifically portrayed, though it is vividly reflected in the Fourth Gospel, where the account of the ministry of Jesus is largely centered about the Temple.

(1) After the Ascension of Jesus the disciples continued in their devotion to the religious life of Ju-

daism, and a large group remained in or near the Temple. From the scene of the Ascension the hundred and twenty who witnessed it returned immediately to Jerusalem (Ac. 1:12). Luke closes his gospel with a summary statement of the activities of the primitive disciples about the Temple. "And they were continually in the Temple, praising God" (Lu. 24:53). The courts of the Temple afforded a general gathering place for the Jerusalem disciples (Ac. 5:12). They continued to take part in the Temple ritual, in which the example was set for them by the two leading apostles, Peter and John, who "were accustomed to go up (imperfect tense in the Greek, signifying customary action) into the Temple at the hour of prayer" (Ac. 3:1). It seemed that the Temple courts afforded them a regular place for teaching (Ac. 4:1; 5:21, 42).

There is no evidence, however, that these early disciples felt themselves bound to the national ritual, the observance of the Jewish feasts and sacred days and seasons. It was the ceremonial requirements of the individual which still maintained a hold upon their consciences (Ac. 3:1; 16:3; 18:18; 21:23-26). This attitude took an extreme form in the agitation of the Judaizers (Ac. 11:2; 15:1).

(2) The early Jewish disciples also held their distinctly Christian services. These were independent of the Temple, or any ceremonial requirement of Judaism (Ac. 1:13; 2:42; 4:23; 12:12). Such gatherings were ordinarily held in the homes of the disciples

(Ac. 2:46; 4:23; 12:12), and, as far as we can infer from later customs, it was a quite prevalent practice to hold such distinctive Christian services on the first day of the week, in commemoration of the Resurrection of Jesus (Ac. 20:7). Nevertheless, we cannot reasonably doubt that the sabbath was still sacred to the Christian Jew.

PHASES OF DEVELOPMENT

There were three disctinct stages in the development of first century Christian life. To interpret the New Testament most effectively, we must follow these three lines of development. This is necessary in order to keep before the student the proper historical perspective, a measure indispensably necessary in accurate interpretation.

(1) *The Ministry of Jesus.* Logically and obviously the first phase of development in New Testament life is the ministry of our Lord. His activity was largely a ministry of benevolent relief for the distress of Palestinian life as it existed in that day, and his teaching was concerned with the practical issues of human experience and the nature and operations of his kingdom. His method and content of propaganda were continued by his first disciples. The message of Jesus is contained in its purest and most original form in the Synoptic Gospels. The Fourth Gospel is not so much a report of the sayings of Jesus as an interpretation of the mind of Jesus, as it was transferred to

JEWISH CHRISTIANITY 21

the Ephesian tradition of the late first century, or was impressed upon the memory of its eye-witness author, and revealed to him in his experience. It appears therefore that the first phase of New Testament interpretation embraces the four Gospels.

(2) *Jewish Christianity.* The second stage of development is the life and thought of Jewish Christianity. Here we find as the earliest and primary norm of activity and teaching the conception of Jesus as the promised Messiah of Israel. In later developments, especially in Hellenistic Jewish Christianity, this conception was expanded to recognize in Jesus the Redeemer of all mankind. It was this modification in the conception which capacitated the Christian message to make contact with the religious mind of the Gentile world. Paganism of that day was entirely familiar with the thought of a divine redeemer. Let the student carefully observe, however, that this universal emphasis was chiefly a product of Hellenistic Jewish Christianity. It was recognized and tolerated in Palestine, but not vigorously promoted. For this reason it is necessary to give separate consideration to *Palestinian Jewish Christianity* and *Hellenistic Jewish Christianity.* The former we shall consider as part one of this commentary, and the latter as part two.

We have observed that our information relative to Palestinian Christianity comes primarily from Acts 1 to 12, with reflections and inferences from the Gospels, particularly the Synoptics. Our study of Hellenistic Jewish Christianity will be based upon intimations from Acts 13 to 28 and a group of epistles.

The oldest and most characteristic of the epistles in this class is James, which is so intensely Jewish that some scholars have denied its Christian origin. A long step away from the epistle of James we find the first Epistle of Peter. But though it is manifestly liberal and cosmopolitan in its tendencies, it has Jewish Christianity chiefly in view, and was written by the pre-eminent Jewish Christian of the Hellenistic world. It is quite specifically addressed to the "elect sojourners of the Dispersion" (1 Pt. 1:1). This phrase is intensely Jewish, in both literary and historical character. Though his Jewish audience frequently blends indistinguishably with its Gentile setting, yet the author never abandons a typically Jewish basis for his argument and appeal. This fact has made parts of the epistle very obscure to Gentile readers. In 2 Peter and Jude Christianity is a universal religion, even though the traditional authors are Jewish Christians. It is impossible to decide with final certainty the questions as to their origin and destination, but they will be treated here on the assumption that they are Jewish messages to Jewish Christians. We will find nothing in the epistles themselves to make that supposition unreasonable, but on the contrary much that will harmonize with such a view. The Epistle to the Hebrews is distinctly and unquestionably a Hellenistic Jewish product. It was written to console the Jewish Christians of a Roman congregation in the face of the complete divorcement of Christianity from Judaism. It is logically and chronologically the culmination of the developments of Jewish Christianity as related to the New Testament. Jewish Christianity continued on into the second century, but in a more and more distorted form. Its treatment there is the province of early church history.

(3) *Gentile Christianity.* In the third stage of development we have the ministry and message of Gentile Christianity. For a considerable period it ran parallel with Jewish Christianity. It contains many Jewish elements, and came chiefly, if not entirely, from Jewish Christian writers, but these writers contemplate Gentile Christianity with their messages, and represent the gospel as it was applied to and interpreted by Gentile Christianity. They show some concern with Jesus as the Messiah of Israel, but their dominant interest is in Jesus as the Redeemer of the world.

The Gentile Christian message divides itself into two great bodies of thought, determined by two great personal influences—Paul and John. The book of Revelation, a part of the Johannine literature, is intensely Jewish in character, material and viewpoint, but without question it contemplates Gentile Christianity as an audience.

We now have the scope of the present discussion before us in its proper historical perspective. It is the second stage in the development of New Testament life. Certain essential distinctions make it necessary to treat Palestinian Jewish Christianity and Hellenistic Jewish Christianity separately. In the first we are concerned chiefly with Acts 1 to 12. In the second we will treat developments of Jewish Christianity in the Gentile world, especially as related to the Epistle of James, I and II Peter and Jude, and the Epistle to the Hebrews.

PART ONE

PALESTINIAN JEWISH CHRISTIANITY

Chapter II

THE GALILEAN DISCIPLES

We have before us here an almost totally neglected phase of primitive Christian history. Yet no phase has been more vital to the formulation and perpetuation of our rich spiritual heritage. We find just here the fountain-head of the blessed tradition which has been transmitted to us in the form of our first three Gospels, especially Matthew and Mark. The discussion of the reasons for considering such to be the origin of our Gospel tradition belongs to the realm of literary critism, and is not in the scope of this discussion, but our purpose here requires that we survey the historical basis for this position.

THE EVIDENCES FOR GALILEAN CHURCHES

While the evidence for these churches is inferential, it is nevertheless quite convincing. There can be no reasonable doubt that there were communities of Christian disciples in Galilee at the dawn of the Apostolic Age. They could have known but little concerning the experiences connected with Pentecost, but they knew the Risen Christ and the good tidings of his redemption.

Several facts point strongly toward this conclusion.

(1) When Jesus departed from Galilee for the Feast of Tabernacles, and eventually the last Pass-

over, there can be no possible doubt that he left multitudes of disciples behind him. It would be unreasonable to suppose that these all deserted him, or forgot their confidence in him. Some of the appearances of the risen Lord were in Galilee, and these would have the effect of reassuring and rallying the Galilean disciples, as those about Jerusalem had revived faith in the Judean disciples. The example and influence of the Jerusalem group would inspire those in Galilee to cling to and perpetuate the message of their Christian hope.

(2) Luke accounts for only a hundred and twenty disciples present at the Ascension and on the day of Pentecost. The total number of disciples was far in excess of this figure. Paul tells us of an appearance of Jesus to "over five hundred brethren" (1 Co. 15:6). If there were only a hundred and twenty present at the Ascension, our safest conclusion is that these five hundred were Galilean disciples. Jesus had certainly promised to meet his disciples in Galilee after the Resurrection (Mk. 14:28), and there are records of specific fulfillments of this promise (Mt. 28:16; Jno. 21:1). Such evidences prove beyond doubt that there were many disciples in Galilee after the Passion of our Lord.

(3) Jews from Galilee were in Jerusalem at Pentecost. We could not safely conclude otherwise than that there were Galileans among the three thousand converted on that occasion. Many of these

JEWISH CHRISTIANITY

would return to Galilee, especially after the earliest messianic excitement had subsided. They would add to the number left by Jesus in Galilee, and would revive their hopes and earnestness.

(4) These disciples were scattered through many villages, towns and cities of Galilee, and under the example and influence of the synagogue they would associate themselves together into communities. As a result there were Jewish Christian churches scattered throughout Galilee. We do not have specific record of these congregations, but we do of other congregations which would most naturally arise as products of Galilean Christianity. On Paul's return journey to Jerusalem after his third missionary journey he found Christian communities at both Tyre and Ptolemais (Ac. 21:4, 7). On his voyage to Rome he was permitted the privilege of visiting Christian friends at Sidon (Ac. 27:3). In 1931 the University of Michigan Institute of Archaeological Research found at Sepphoris the remains of an ancient Christian church.

None of these evidences is conclusive in itself, but together they make a cumulative argument which is sufficient to convince us beyond reasonable doubt that in the early Apostolic Age there were Galilean churches.

LIFE IN THE GALILEAN CHURCHES

The distinction between the Galilean churches and the Judean churches was geograpical rather than essential. The former knew of the Ascension and the Pentecostal experiences only by report, but without doubt they accepted these fundamental historical events and predicated their own experience upon them. They would still respect Jerusalem as the rightful center of Messianic propagation and expectation. As we seek to discern these primitive Galilean disciples in the background of the Synoptic Gospels, we may detect certain probabilities relative to their community life, and form inferences as to their personal life.

(1) *Community Life.* We cannot do otherwise than suppose that these disciples did associate themselves in a rather definite community life. This community life was fashioned after the Jewish synagogue, and doubtless designated by the same name, *moedh* or *kenishta*. By means of this community life discipline was maintained and fellowship promoted. This fellowship was closely guarded, because it was an essential factor in the life and progress of the churches.

The community assemblies quite likely followed the general custom of synagogue services, yet differing at many points. The Scriptures would be read at the services, but the Christians gave a much larger place to the Prophets and Hagiographa than did the Jews. The traditional synagogue liturgy would be largely discarded. Instead of the familiar Jewish ritual of confession, the "Shema", the Christian assemblies would repeat in unison the Lord's Prayer. One would hear in

JEWISH CHRISTIANITY

the Galilean congregation the Matthean version of it. A shorter version prevailed in the Judean churches, and was recorded by Luke. There would be the customary exhortation and teaching, but instead of rabbinic tradition they used the traditions of the deeds and sayings of Jesus. These would naturally be adapted to the existing needs of individual and community life. Experiences in the home, in social and church relations, or even in economic and business relations, would raise questions for which answers would be found in the teaching of Jesus.

These community assemblies were doubtless at first held on the Jewish sabbath, turning more and more to the first day of the week under Judean influence. Evangelical Christian faith contemplates the Holy Spirit as overshadowing the entire process.

The Christian community in Galilee had much in common with their Jewish neighbors. They used the same Scriptures, claimed the same national heritage, and followed in many respects the same religious practices. It is even highly probable that they continued to attend the synagogue, at least occasionally. But there existed two characteristic distinctions between the Christian and non-Christian Jews.

i. The chief distinction lay in the fact that the Christian Jews constituted a Messianic rather than a rabbinic community. The scribes or rabbis dominated the synagogue life, and they had no very deep interest in the Messianic hope, and were confused and at variance in their teaching on the point. Their religious life and instruction revolved about the Law and its traditional interpretation. The faith of the Galilean Christian community centered in the Messiahship of Jesus. His historical life and character defined for them a Messianism widely different from that of rabbinic Judaism. Jesus was a teaching Messiah and a suffering Messiah—characteristics radically variant from prevailing Jewish conceptions. It was this distinctive Messianism which constituted the chief line of demarcation setting apart the Christian community.

ii. There was a spiritual emphasis and enthusiasm which was strikingly different from ordinary Judaism. The Christian Jews were distinguished by the ardour of their faith and their exultant confidence in the truth and ultimate triumph of their cause. This spirit possessed a potent appeal to those about them, and was one of their strongest means of winning recruits for their movement.

If we are accurately to picture a Galilean church of 35 A. D., we must contemplate a group of Christian Jews, living in a Galilean town, meeting perhaps weekly in the home which could best accomodate them, having only a very loose and varying form of organization, devoting themselves to perpetuating the memory of Jesus and his teaching, hoping for his early return, and exultantly enthusiastic in their Messianic faith. The materials for the construction of this picture are confessedly inferential and speculative, but at least we have evidence enough to convince us that a picture different from this could not claim any historical probability.

(2) *Personal Life.* Personal life was so thoroughly interwoven with community life that many of its features have been involved in the foregoing discussion. But there are yet other features of Galilean Christianity which may be contemplated as distinctively personal. Much of the teaching of our Lord which these primitive disciples preserved for us bears out this supposition.

The Sermon on the Mount is the most practical, most sublime program of personal conduct ever offered. Those German scholars who would have us suppose that the early Palestinian churches devised these transcendent ideals and put them in the mouth of Jesus, gathering them around a slight nucleus of genuine sayings, are placing too great a strain on our credulity. That those primitive Jewish Christians could have created such exalted conceptions of life is not conceivable. The only mind in the first century world capable of those teachings was the mind of their divine Master. Their part was to recall, and formulate into tradition, the things he had said, as the exigencies of experience presented a demand for them. The preservation of this great discourse was not accidental, nor merely supernatural. The divine Spirit first recalled its ideals in the memory of the Galilean disciples (cf. John 14:26), and then applied them in daily life. Luke records a shorter version, as preserved in Judean tradition. One who maintains a spiritual attitude toward life and history can but see in these processes the benevolent provision of a divine plan.

In personal life there were persecution and privation to suffer. The early Galilean disciples were confronted with the opposition of their countrymen. Rabbinic censure and Pharisaic bigotry were constantly harassing them. Boycott and ostracism likely faced them in some localities. Economic destitution was the ordinary status of a Galilean Christian community. Paul's collection for the "poor saints" (1 Co. 16:2, etc.) was not necessarily confined to the Judean believers; at least there can be no reasonable doubt that there were Galilean disciples who were in need of such help, for their plight was comparable to that of the Judean Christians. These situations of life were met with the Master's instructions. Messages of their Lord on the cold formalism of rabbinic Judaism and Pharisaic hypocrisy were used to reassure the disciples and refute their opponents. With tender gratitude and returning hope would they recall those comforting words, "Come unto me, all ye that labor and are heavy laden, and I will give you rest" (Mt. 11:28). Privations could be endured with becoming fortitude when they were reminded of the treasures laid up in heaven (Mt. 6:19f.) and the compassion of the Shepherd for the scattered sheep (Mt. 9:36). These kindly words of the Great Teacher soothed the distraught hearts of men for many years before they were permanently inscribed for the blessing of future generations. In the Master's teaching the first believers found encouragement and exhortation in life's emergencies.

Reflection and investigation will serve to increase the sense of certainty that the picture here constructed from inferential materials is in approximate accord with the facts of life in Galilean Christianity between 30 and 50 A. D. Such an historical reconstruction offers a reasonable explanation of many literary and factual developments, and detracts in no way from a most earnestly religious view of this period of history as part of a redemptive plan. We are but searching more thoroughly into the historical processes employed by the divine Spirit in revelation.

Chapter III

THE JUDEAN DISCIPLES

Just as we have in Judea the heart of Judaism so also we have the influential center of Jewish Christianity. Judean Christian life revolved around Jerusalem, and even the Galilean disciples respected Jerusalem as the necessary and rightful center of Messianic teaching and expectation.

The materials in hand define three phases for the discussion of this topic. They are the development of the early Judean churches, the methods employed in administering the affairs of early Jerusalem Christianity, and the means adopted in providing temporal support. For the first phase of the discussion we have only inferential light from Acts and the Synoptic tradition. The other two matters are definitely treated in the book of Acts, and may be considered on much more secure grounds than the prior discussion has been able to offer.

THE EARLY JUDEAN CHURCHES

The book of Acts gives us the record of only those disciples who tarried in Jerusalem. Just as we have felt convinced from strong inferential evidence that there were churches in Galilee from the time of the Resurrection, so we find reason to believe that there were separate congregations in Judea, outside Jerusalem. We would offer three grounds for this conclusion.

JEWISH CHRISTIANITY

(1) *Intrinsic Probability.* We have before us here the same natural inferences which we observed relative to the Galilean disciples. It is important to bear in mind that Luke mentions a hundred and twenty as the number of the disciples who were assembled in Jerusalem before Pentecost. The implication is that this was the total number of believers tarrying at that time in Jerusalem. We can hardly suppose that these constituted the entire number of Judean disciples. In all probability there were several times this number. Then among the three thousand who accepted the Messiahship of Jesus at Pentecost there were of course many Jews from outside Jerusalem, from Judea as well as Galilee. Numbers of these had returned to their homes. These disciples, scattered through the towns and villages of Judea, would inevitably cohere in some form of community life. As a result we have Judean churches.

Though these inferences are purely hypothetical, they have an intrinsic probability which makes them very convincing. Then there are other evidences more direct and objective. (Cf. Gal. 1.22; I Thes. 2:14.)

(2) *Church Life In Jerusalem.* Luke gives us a picture of life in Jerusalem Christianity which strongly suggests an analogy in Judean Christian life. Acts 2:46 is a passage most remarkable for its vivid suggestiveness. It is Luke's summary of the religious life of the Jerusalem church at this period. There are in this verse two points of special historical significance.

(i) Luke describes the Jerusalem disciples as "daily with one accord waiting patiently in the Temple". For what were they waiting? Doubtless they waited in the hope that the Messiah might soon return to the Temple in which he had manifested so much interest during his earthly life. At any rate, we are informed here that every day a group of the disciples tarried in the Temple courts.

(ii) But not all the disciples were in the Temple. The great majority were "breaking bread from house to house". The phrase rendered "at home" by the Am. St. Version, is better rendered by the Authorized Version, which reads, "from house to house". This is a vivid and significant description. The Christian disciples had no synagogues. Outside the Temple courts they had access to no regular meeting place. Consequently, they met in groups in various homes large enough to accomodate them. Especially were they accustomed to meet together in such household assemblies for meals. The meal was a sacred affair in the Jewish home. It had a religious significance. Many disciples from outside Jerusalem were dependent upon their Jerusalem brethren for support. Those who were able were entertaining the others at meals. These gatherings around the table board took on an unusual religious significance for the Christian Jews. They became distinctively religious assemblies. In these groups they would discuss their faith in Jesus, their hope of his return, and their recollections of his earthly life and teachings. In these group meetings there began the formulation of traditions which have come to us in our Gospel records.

The Jerusalem disciples exerted a strong influence over the disciples in Judea. The latter would naturally emulate the example of the Jerusalem believers, and adopt the custom of holding household meetings, and with them the chief materials for discussion would be the traditions concerning Jesus. It is safe to suppose that the picture Luke presents to us of the Jerusalem disciples may be extended out into Judea.

(3) *Dispersion of the Jerusalem Disciples.* How long the disciples in Jerusalem remained unmolested we cannot tell. It is extremely probable that it was not for long—a few months at most. Persecution was first inflicted by the Temple authorities, who were mainly Sadducees; but it was not very severe at their hands. But when the Pharisees became aroused, and slashed out at the infant Jewish Christian church, many of the disciples were forced to take refuge in flight, "and were all scattered abroad throughout the regions of Judea and Samaria" (Ac. 8:1). It is likely that these fleeing disciples found Christian communities already established in Judea and Samaria to which they might attach themselves—at least in Judea; but however that may be, here is documentary attestation of an early distribution of Christian disciples through Judea and Samaria.

There is further evidence in Acts that these disciples gathered together in communities, or "churches", and that such communities extended into Galilee. After the conversion of Saul, the arch-persecutor, we are told that, "the churches had peace throughout all Judea and Galilee and Samaria" (Ac. 9:31). The revisers' text, represented in the Am. St. Version, has the singular "church", and is supported in this reading by the great majority of the manuscripts, both early and late; but all our extant manuscripts of the New Testament were produced under strong ecclesiastical influence, and this reading is thoroughly in harmony with ecclesiastical conceptions. We believe that on grounds of intrinsic and transcriptional probability the plural may be accepted as the correct reading. But however that may be in either reading plain testimony is borne to the fact that Jewish Christianity was spread throughout Judea, Samaria and Galilee at the time of the conversion of Saul; and, of course, as far as Damascus, for it was to disperse the Christian assembly there that Saul was on his way when converted.

The cumulative force of the evidences canvassed convinces us that from the time of the Resurrection Jewish Christian communities existed in Judea and Galilee, and probably in Samaria. We may vizualize the life of the Judean congregations as very similar to that already described for Galilee. Traditions relative to the Master were utilized for teaching and exhortation in their assemblies, and the Lord's

Prayer was used, though in a shorter form than that employed in Galilee (cf. Lu. 11:2-4). The Judean Christians, like their Galilean brethren, were harassed by scribism and Pharisaism. They were experiencing a severe struggle with economic privation, so that they needed the comfort of such messages of the Master as the parable of the Rich Fool, and of the Rich Man and Lazarus; and eventually appealed to the sympathetic concern of Paul and were a matter of anxiety to the leading apostles at Jerusalem (Gal. 2:10). We infer from the Gospel sources that women were much more active in the Judean Christian communities than in the synagogues of Judaism. Two sisters like Mary and Martha could take a prominent place in Judean Christianity because they had held a position of honor and respect in the inner circle of the associates of Jesus, and doubtless also upon their own essential merits. There existed a cordial fellowship, alien to Judaism, between the Judean and Samaritan disciples, so that the Judean disciples would find satisfaction in repeating Jesus' parable of the Good Samaritan, and would preserve the story of the founding of Samaritan Christianity through the conversion of an outcast woman.

We have before us now a conjectural, but certainly approximate picture of the cradle of apostolic Christianity and fountain-head of Gospel tradition. Henceforth we confine ourselves to the documentary evidences of the book of Acts.

Methods of Administration

Acts i. 15-26; vi. 1-6; xv. 1-29

As we first observe the policy of administration in Jerusalem it is necessarily provisional and transitional, because the community was in a plastic and unsettled state. Permanent principles of church government were incipient here, and reached full development later. The methods of organization which we find in the later Pauline churches, particularly as reflected in the Pastoral Epistles, are advanced far beyond these primitive beginnings. But the church must have beginnings in both message and constitution.

(1) The apostles, as the divinely appointed leaders and guardians, held the chief direction of affairs in early Jewish Christianity, especially in the earliest life at Jerusalem. This of course was inevitable. The apostles had had personal contact with Christ; they possessed a mighty influence over all the primitive disciples, in and outside Jerusalem; the people were untrained, and had no conception as yet of the plan or necessity of permanent organization; the authority of the apostles was taken by common consent as directly from the risen Lord, and therefore final. It was expected that the Messiah would speedily return to the earth for the consummation of his kingdom, and therefore any form of organization was provisional: no permanent form of organization was thought necessary. It is interesting that in Acts 1:17, 20, 25 we find the office of the apostles designated

by the Greek words for apostle, bishop and deacon. At that period they functioned in all three capacities.

(2) The voice of the people was recognized and given a part in the government. This is clearly reflected in the incident recorded in 1:15-26. The Lord had chosen twelve apostles. This fact naturally caused the disciples to feel that the place left vacant by the treason and suicide of Judas should be filled again. Futhermore, the number eleven was intolerable to a Jew. Hence Peter reminds the assembled disciples, a hundred and twenty in number, that necessity is upon them to supply the vacant apostolate. It is significant that Peter declined to assume authority to make the appointment, and did not call on the eleven apostles to choose a successor for Judas. Instead, he arose in the midst of the assembled disciples, and called on the entire group to select a successor to Judas.

The matter was done in strictly Jewish fashion. By some method not described by Luke common agreement was reached that two disciples, Joseph Barsabbas, and Matthias, should be presented to the Lord for Him to make divine choice. The method employed for determining this divine choice was the casting of lots. The fact that this is the last record we have of the casting of lots to determine God's will reminds us how quickly Christianity changed from a Jewish to a Greek religion. The Greeks, with their greater intellectual progress, had long ago abandoned this mode of decision. Probably the names of the two candidates were inscribed on small cubes of wood or other material, these cubes placed in a bowl, and the bowl whirled rapidly until the centrifugal action caused a block to be thrown from the bowl. The first name thus cast from the bowl was the one upon whom the choice rested.

The point of special note is that the procedure was subject to the will of the entire group, rather than to the apostles, or any one apostle. Where Luke says of Matthias that "he was numbered with the eleven apostles" (vs. 26), the word rendered "number" really means, according to Thayer (*Greek-English Lexicon of the N. T.*, s. v.), "to vote one a place among". So what Luke wrote was, "He was voted a place among the eleven apostles". Luke's knowledge of the incident caused him to regard Matthias as obtaining his office by the choice of the entire group of the assembled disciples.

The same principle is evident in the selection of the Seven (Ac. 6:1-6). An embarassing emergency had arisen in the life of the Jerusalem church. Among the Jews from outside Palestine—the "Grecian Jews" referred to in verse 1—who had been won to Chirst on Pentecost and thereafter, were a number of widows. In the administration of the Jerusalem church, these widows had been deliberately neglected. The Palestinian Jews, or "Hebrews" as they are here called, looked with considerable aversion upon the Hellenistic Jews. The Hellenistic Jews lived in the unclean

Gentile world, and not in "The Land", as the Palestinian Jew fondly called his home-land of divine promise and sacred tradition. They were in perpetual contact with Gentiles, and inevitably felt more lenient toward the heathen than the strict Judean Jew. Hence the Judean would look upon them as a lower class, and unworthy of the same high privileges and generous consideration which would rightfully be accorded a Palestinian Jew. Hence, when the charity funds became depleted, it was considered by the Jerusalem Christians, among whom Palestinian Jews were greatly in the majority, that it was nothing more than logical and right that the Hellenistic widows should be the first dropped from the lists of church support. But such prejudiced discrimination quite naturally provoked complaint from the Hellenistic Jewish Christians.

The situation demanded immediate action. Wise personal supervision appeared clearly to be the only adequate solution. But for the Apostles to take the matter in hand would encroach too much on the time which they needed to devote to the spiritual life of the church. They therefore decided that the wise plan would be to put the matter in the hands of a group of strong, practical men, who could devote themselves entirely to this one problem. It is significant, however, that they did not assume authority to appoint these helpers, but called the church into conference, and laid upon them the responsibility of the choice. We may reasonably suppose that the Apostles recommended the Seven, and the record specifically tells us that the Apostles ordained them, but their selection was left to the voice of the people.

It appears that an adjustment was made that was calculated to give perfect satisfaction to the complaining Hellenists, for all seven of the new officials bore Greek names, and one was a Gentile proselyte to the Jewish religion who had formerly lived in the intensely Greek city of Antioch. Thus the interests of the Hellenistic Jews were entirely safeguarded. Nevertheless, we cannot conclude with certainty that the six Jews with Greek names were necessarily Hellenists, for so great was the Hellenistic influence in Palestine itself that many Palestinian parents gave their children Greek names, probably ignorant of the racial origin of such names. But at least the Greek names indicate the presence among the Seven of a sufficient Hellenistic sympathy.

These seven officials are frequently described as deacons, but the record in Acts does not designate them by this word, at least in its noun form. It does define their function by the verb from the same root as the noun which the English New Testament tranliterates "deacon" (Greek, *diaconos*), but the verb is simply the regular Greek word for serve or minister, and consequently too much cannot be inferred from it. However, in the absence of any evidence to the contrary, it is not unreasonable to regard them as the

JEWISH CHRISTIANITY 47

first deacons, and by way of convenience to call them such.

The policy thus adopted by the church upon the recommendation of the Apostles operated with abundant success. Many new believers were added to the church, and even Sadducaic priests turned with more favorable attention to this rapidly growing movement, and many of them espoused the new faith.

(3) Elders were added to the church organization somewhere between the time of the selection of the Seven and the events recorded in the latter part of the eleventh chapter of Acts (11:27-30). About A. D. 45 there came a severe famine in Palestine, and since the Jerusalem disciples were already in economic straits, due to the excessive burdens they had assumed after Pentecost in undertaking the support of all those who had been converted from among the visitors at the Feast, the famine placed them in a tragic situation. But providential aid had been provided. One of their own prophets had gone to Antioch and there given warning of the approaching famine, so that a fund had been subscribed by the church there for the destitute saints at Jerusalem. This relief fund is described by Luke as a "ministry," the same word used in connection with the appointment of the Seven, so we would expect it to be placed in charge of the deacons, but instead we are told that it was sent to the elders. So there had arisen in the Jerusalem church a new group of officials called elders.

The exact occasion and appointment of these elders we do not know. They probably arose to take the place of the Apostles, as the latter were more and more called away from Jerusalem to minister to other communities. From the revised text of Acts 9:31,32 it is evident that all the Christians in Judea, Samaria and Galilee were regarded as attached to the original Jerusalem church, and that the Apostles journeyed about to minister to them. Only Peter and John are mentioned specifically as engaged in this itinerant work, but it is hardly to be supposed that only these two cared for the interests of the scattered congregations of Palestine. It is more probable that all twelve of the Apostles went on these itinerancies, and that the elders had charge of affairs in Jerusalem during their absence.

(4) Eventually James the half-brother of Jesus became the dominant figure in the Jerusalem church, and in Jewish Christianity generally. He was probably among the elders chosen by the church, but, due to his own merit and capability and his relation to Jesus, he rapidly forged to the front until he became the leading personality in the church, accepted in both function and title as an apostle.

That he exercised the function of apostleship may be seen in the fifteenth chapter of Acts (15:1-29). Here he appears on a par with Peter in authority and influence. It is the occasion of the Jerusalem Council, when the church at Antioch sent a request to the church at Jerusalem to advise them as to the attitude of the mother church on the question of requiring circumcision of the Gentiles who became Christians. Here a new stage of advancement appears in the development of church administration in Jerusalem. It is now both the Apostles and elders who take the lead in affairs, doubtless with James as the dominant apostolic leader. The situation we find now is James as preeminent, with Peter still in a prominent place, the Apostles and elders associated closely together in the administration, while the voice of the church is still recognized in the final settlement of affairs.

When the church was called in conference Peter was the first to address himself to the question, probably due to his personal traits rather than his superior influence. Paul and Barnabas then presented the case as they saw it. Finally, at the most crucial moment in the discussion, James arose and announced his view of the matter. His was clearly the deciding voice. Immediately the church took action to follow the course James had proposed. In describing the same incident in Galatians (2:6-10) Paul associates James with Peter and John in such way that it is obvious he was considered as on an equal footing with them. In Gal. 1:19 Paul intimates that at Jerusalem James was accorded the title of apostle, though we may safely assume that he was not regarded as exactly in a class with the Twelve. Let it be distinctly borne in mind, however, that James was never the "pastor" of the Jerusalem church. The church at Jerusalem had a number of pastors, or elders, and James was likely first the most influential of these elders, having finally attained to the place of apostolic leader of the church and the most influential personality in Jewish Christianity.

THE PROBLEM OF TEMPORAL SUPPORT

Acts 2:42-47; 4:32-5:11

Because of the emergency which presented itself following Pentecost, and the policies adopted in meeting it, the matter of temporal support in the early apostolic group calls for separate discussion. The economic problem was met by drastic measures. There was a practically unanimous movement on the part of those who had property or merchantable goods to dispose of their assets and provide for the entire group. Thus they supported themselves by a voluntary community of goods.

We will consider now the causes and progress of this revolutionary policy. There were three probable causes.

(1) The great majority of the disciples had their homes and usual means of livelihood far from Jerusalem. Among them were the original disciples from Galilee, who had no regular source of support in Jerusalem. Then there probably remained in Jerusalem many of the converts made at Pentecost from

JEWISH CHRISTIANITY 51

among the Jews of the Dispersion (Ac. 2:9-11). These two classes together constituted a large group who were dependent upon the generosity of friends for support.

(2) It was a time of serious economic depression and widespread poverty, so that many of the disciples were likely already in a state of material destitution.

(3) They were looking for the early return of Jesus, and therefore regarded any permanent adjustment of economic needs as unnecessary. It was Jerusalem Christianity which had most influenced Paul, and a remote reflection of the intense anticipation of the early return of the Messiah survives in 1 Co. 16-22, *Maran atha,* which is Aramaic for, "Our Lord is coming." The fact of this expression being in Aramaic indicates its origin among Palestinian disciples. They hoped the Messiah might return any day, and if he did, they expected he would return to the courts of his Temple. Some provisional arrangement which would take care of the immediate emergency they considered sufficient. The property or money contributed would be freely parted with, for they hoped the Messiah would soon return to establish his eternal kingdom, and then earthly wealth would be superflous. A Messiah who could feed more than five thousand people with five loaves and two fishes would bring the solution of all their economic problems. It seems that for a time they abandoned the ordinary

pursuits of life, and gave themselves wholly to religious exercise. In this state of life and attitude of mind any temporary arrangement for material support would be satisfactory.

This practice of community of goods first appears in Ac. 2:43-47. The Greek text of this passage indicates that there was no rash disposal of all merchantable property or donation of all available capital immediately, but from time to time, as the need arose, sales were made and provisions secured. The meals were served in various homes of disciples who lived in Jerusalem. As observed above, the phrase in verse 46 rendered in the American Standard Version, "breaking bread at home," is better rendered in the Authorized Version, "breaking bread from house to house." The generosity and devotion exhibited by this policy made a profound impression, and as the disciples continued their religious services and teaching in the Gentiles Court of the Temple, many more believers were added to their number.

The next view which Luke gives us of the progress of this novel economic program is in Ac. 4:32-5:11. Here it was revived with even more gratifying success, but eventually produced developments which were far from satisfactory. There had been a fresh enduement of the Spirit, and an unusual spirit of unity prevailed. Luke places special emphasis on this spirit of unity. Verse 32 literally reads, "Now the multitude of believers were heart and soul one." This spirit of harmony produced two significant results. The first was a sense of stewardship on the part of the entire church membership: "and not one said that anything he possessed was his own." The enduement of the Holy Spirit brought perfect harmony, and the Holy Spirit operating upon the hearts of a unified church brought a stewardship revival. Then the second result of this Spirit-wrought harmony was a religious revival (verse 37). After thus briefly summarizing the results the writer goes on to describe in more detail the generosity of the revived church. Modern critics have regarded this benevolent enterprise of the Jerusalem church as a stupid blunder of overzealous religionists, but plainly Luke did not share their attitude. He gives it a prominence which unquestionably implies his hearty sanction. In the passage before us, as in the second chapter, the Greek suggests that the sale of property was made from time to time as members of the congregation felt the pinch of poverty. The verbs are in the imperfect tense —most probably the iterative imperfect: "they brought from time to time;" "they laid from time to time;" "from time to time distribution was made to each, as anyone had need."

A conspicuous case was that of Joseph, who already had so distinguished himself in his helpful ministries to those in need that they had nicknamed him "son of helpfulness." At least this is the best rendering of the Greek of this passage, though there is great doubt surrounding the meaning of the Aramiac word for Barnabas. This is without doubt the Barnabas who was the helpful companion of Paul on the latter's first missionary journey. He was of priestly descent, and a native of Cyprus. That the field he sold represented the total of his possessions we are not told, but such is the inference.

Such benevolence as that of Barnabas was held in high honor by the church. Two other members were looking covetously at this honor but were unwilling to pay the price of impoverishing themselves for the sake of their needy brethern. Their inordinate ambition and selfish greed led to a disgraceful tragedy. Ananias and Sapphira both met death as the penalty of their hypocrisy.

This horrible incident is a baffling problem to refined Christian sensibilities. The easy way out of the problem is to deny the historicity of it. But in that assumption one faces a yet more difficult problem: how could such a tradition ever have arisen if it had no basis in fact? And accepted as a fact it is not without its rational explanation. It is to be interpreted in the light of four important considerations.

(1) Ananias was under no compulsion to sell any of his property, nor to bring any of the price to the common treasury. We have no compulsory communism here. Peter quite definitely reminds Ananias, "While it remained, did it not remain thine own? and after it was sold, was it not in thy power?" This ghastly deed was entirely voluntary.

(2) The scheme of Ananias was diabolical in its dishonesty. He had planned to fraudulently secure the honor and appreciation of the church by leading them to suppose that he had brought all the proceeds of his property to the common treasury. By unfair means he sought to secure access to the common storehouse, for having delivered, as would be supposed, all his resources to the Apostles, he would of necessity be dependent upon the church for support. Then he could lay away part of the sale price which he retained, and be maintained by the charity of the church. The whole scheme was intensely selfish and shockingly hypocritical.

(3) The church was in its infancy. Any serious disruption or betrayal now could so easily issue in desparate consequences. Any attempt at defection must be checked promptly and decisively. Hence drastic measures were not only justifiable but indispensable. As a parent would repel with violent means the attempt of a murderous hand to harm a helpless babe, so the divine Spirit laid crushing judgment upon an effort to betray with perfidy the infant church. That such judgments were never again used is to be explained by the simple fact that they were never again needed.

(4) Peter did not in the first instance pronounce any curse upon the wrong-doers, but when he had seen the terrific judgment of God fall upon Ananias he was forced to infer that a like judgment was

deserved by his wife. The immediate burial of Ananias was a circumstance made necessary by the climate of Judea. That Sapphira was ignorant of the tragic fate of her husband is doubtless to be explained by the excitement and bewilderment which followed his death—no one had thought of being responsible for notifying the wife. When she finally approached the gathered throng, everyone in horror held his peace, and waited to see the outcome. By a wisely constructed question Peter ascertained that she was guilty with her husband of the dastardly treachery and hypocrisy. Deducing from the fate of her husband the necessity for a similar curse upon her, Peter pronounced the fearful judgment. The entire church felt the shock of the tragic incident.

It appears that there came later an attempt to restore the normal economic adjustment, when charity was dispensed only to special cases of need. Then as a natural development those able to make a living for themselves would gradually secure their own sources of support, leaving to the charity of the church only those cases where independent support was impossible. From Ac. 6:1 we infer that only the destitute widows were being cared for by the church at that time. But at a later period famine afflicted the land, and destitution again prevailed among the Jewish Christians, calling forth the benevolence of the church at Antioch, as described in Ac. 11:29,30. The persistence of such a situation is probably reflected in Gal.

JEWISH CHRISTIANITY

2:10, where Paul and Barnabas covenant with the Jerusalem apostles to help them with the care of the poor. The offering which Paul later secured from a number of the Gentile churches was for poverty-stricken disciples in the same locality (cf. Rom. 15: 26; 1 Co. 16:1-3; 2 Co. 8:1-9:15).

This state of extreme privation which prevailed so long among the Christians of Palestine arose from four interactive causes.

(1) There was general economic destitution existing throughout Palestine and affecting all its inhabitants. The excess of population, combined with Jewish prejudice against all Gentile contacts and disfavor toward barter and trade in general, had greatly impoverished the Palestinian Jews of the first century.

(2) A state of political unrest and confusion made living conditions difficult. The Jews of Palestine, aggravated especially by the Zealots, were irreconcilably opposed to the Roman regime, and more and more this opposition was breaking out in active rebellion. Such conditions could only augment the economic distress.

(3) The suffering of the Christian Jews was increased by the persecution inflicted upon them at the hands of the anti-Christian Jews. They were subjected to boycott and ostracism, which of course intensified the already existing difficulty of securing temporal support.

(4) After about 45 A. D. a succession of famines wrought great distress and dire want in Palestine. The Christian Jews, already seriously impoverished, probably suffered extreme hunger and privation during this period. Their sad plight appealed to the generosity of Paul and his Gentile churches.

The results of these combined causes was an economic situation which brought excessive poverty and suffering to the Palestinian Christians. It is probable that until the time of the Jewish revolt of A. D. 66-70 the Jerusalem and Judean disciples suffered serious material destitution, and their leaders were forced to maintain methods of charitable support.

Chapter IV

THE MESSAGE OF PALESTINIAN CHRISTIANITY

Within a short while after Jesus left his disciples they became impressed with an irresistable sense of duty to proclaim the message of his Messianic mission. They discoursed upon it in their distinctive gatherings from house to house, and proclaimed it in the courts of the Temple. Probably they also preached as far as they were allowed in the public square and synagogue of Palestinian towns, and in household assemblies. What they called this message at the beginning we cannot even guess, but Paul called it the *euangellion*, "good tidings", and his designation won general acceptance in the Hellenistic Christian world and has come down to the present time, being represented in our English word gospel. The original Aramaic designation might have been akin to it. But by whatever name the message was at first known, from the very beginning there was an indomitable impulse to proclaim that message to others. Any historical inquiry into these early years of Christian history must find an explanation for this undoubted phenomenon. The Acts account presents an adequate hypothesis, objectionable only to one who finds himself unable to accept the supernatural.

THE DYNAMIC OF THE MESSAGE
Ac. 1:1-14; 2:1-13; 4:23-31

The general outline of the history recorded in the first eleven chapters of Acts is now accepted as authentic even by extremely liberal critics. But these facts must have a rational explanation. Such results must have an adequate cause. That cause is disclosed in Ac. 1:1-14; 2:1-42; 4:23-37. Here there is described the coming of the Holy Spirit and the resultant impetus given the gospel propaganda in its incipiency.

(1) *The Promise of the Dynamic* (1:1-11). This is for Luke the very first point of interest in apostolic history. It constitutes the climax in the opening sentence of the book. In a very concise introduction Luke sets forth as the purpose of his "former treatise"—the third gospel—to narrate the establishment or inauguration of the kingdom of God on earth by the Lord himself, his earthly ministry culminating in his passion, resurrection, appearances, commission to his apostles, and ascension. All this is summarized in a single sentence, which reaches its climax in a description of the promise of the Holy Spirit (cf. 1:1-5). Thus Luke thrusts before the reader in the very opening of the book of Acts the dynamic of the expanding kingdom.

The promise of the Spirit is the supreme concern of the disciple of Christ. This is the emphatic point in 1:6-11. The assembled disciples were still concerned with their age-long Jewish hope. They yearned that the throne of David might be re-established in the earth, and Israel might be restored to his former glory and elevated to the supreme place among the nations. Their political conception of the Messianic kingdom had not been wholly abandoned—was not until Pentecost. Jesus assures them that the matter into which they are now inquiring is not at all their concern. The time and circumstances of the consummation of the kingdom of God on earth is to be kept within God's authority. Their concern is not for the political power of a Messianic kingdom, but the spiritual power of an enduing Spirit. Their task is not to subject the world to a Messianic king, but to witness to the world for a risen Redeemer.

Having, as a parting instruction, made this supreme interest clear to the disciples, Jesus was gently lifted for a short distance above the earth, and then the fleecy folds of a silvery cloud gathered their silken draperies about his resurrection form and caught him away from the sight of mortal man. All the quibblings and carpings about the cosmic problems of the Ascension are smothered in the feathery folds of that cloud. In like clouds of inscrutable mystery he will return to earth again.

(2) *The Preparation For the Dynamic* (1:12-14). Three elements constituted this preparation. (i) In verse 12 we find submission to the will of Christ. He had commanded them to tarry in the city until they should be clothed with power from on high (Lu. 24:49). In obedience to this command they returned to Jerusalem. (Cf. 5:32.) (ii) Verse 13 shows their faith in the promise. Upon their arrival in the city they repaired to the upper room which some generous disciple had tendered to the apostles as a lodging place

while they were in Jerusalem. Confident that the Savior's promise would be fulfilled, they settled themselves here to wait. The verb rendered "they were abiding" is in the imperfect tense. We construe it as an inceptive imperfect, and would render it, "where they began waiting." They had faith enough to wait for ten days. (Cf. Gal. 3:14.) (iii) Verse 14 presents prayer as a preparation for the dynamic. Note the unusual emphasis placed by Luke upon this prayer meeting. To have said simply, "These prayed", would have recorded the fact. But Luke piles one upon another four devises of emphasis. "These *all–with one accord - continued - steadfastly* in prayer." The Greek literally means they devoted themselves persistently to prayer. It is not accidental that Luke thus emphasizes this prayer meeting. He was conscious of its relation to the fulfillment of the promise, which fulfillment he records in the second chapter of Acts.

(3) *Enduement With the Dynamic* (2:1-13). There are few other passages in the Bible beclouded with more confusion than are these verses. And upon reflection we realize that that is not a strange fact at all. There is no passage in the Bible which Satan could desire more to have misunderstood. There is nothing on this earth which can do more damage to the devices of the evil one than a redeemed life filled with the Holy Spirit. Hence the devil would quite naturally wish to veil this revelation in all the distortion and misinterpretation that his diabolical ingenuity can manufacture.

JEWISH CHRISTIANITY

There is not space here to review the many and conflicting interpretations offered for this vital passage—and if there were space it would not be wise to thus waste it. The basal principle by which a correct interpretation must be guided is to distinguish between the temporary and the essential elements in this passage. There are certain elements which were called for by the exigencies of the immediate occasion. The "sound as of a mighty wind rushing along" which filled the entire house in which the assembled disciples occupied the upper room, and the "tongues distributed about like flames of fire", were tangible phenomena which were granted these primitive disciples to attest to them the reality and genuineness of their experience. They were at the incipiency of the kingdom enterprise, and needed that a tangible demonstration be given them that they might have no question that the promise of Christ had been fulfilled. When once the experience was fully established and authenticated such tangible demonstrations were not needed. For that reason they do not attend the experience today, and have not since the early days of the Apostolic Age.

And not only did the disciples need a tangible evidence of the Spirit's power, but His advent must needs be attested to the people to whom they were to to proclaim Christ's redemptive message. Consequently, they were endowed with a supernatural power of speech, whereby they could address all the visitors at the Feast, assembled from all quarters of the Roman world, in the various dialects with which they were familiar in their native lands. To hear these Galileans thus speak in several dialects filled the gathered throngs with wonder, and opened their hearts and minds for the reception of the gospel message.

But there was that in this experience which was essential and permanent. By Jesus and John the Baptist it was described as a baptism (Mt. 3:11; Ac. 1:5). By Paul and Luke it was described as an infilling (Ac. 2:4; Eph. 5:18). Viewed under the figure of a baptism, it was that complete overwhelming of the lives of the disciples by the power of the divine Spirit which made them absolutely His possession. As an infilling, it was the complete permeation of their hearts and lives whereby the Holy Spirit influenced and determined their every thought and action. He completely possessed them and freely used them. To be possessed by the Spirit and used by the Spirit are the essential elements of the experience, the elements which abide to our own day and shall continue to the consummation of the kingdom.

(4) *Results of the Dynamic*. The results were twofold. It produced an evangelistic revival (2:5-42) and a stewardship revival (4:31-37). In the first revival Peter preached the gospel with surpassing power, and three thousand were added to the kingdom. In the second revival "with great power gave the apostles their witnesses" (4:33), and as a result the multitude of the disciples devoted their material means to the

needs of the kingdom with unstinted liberality. Thus the coming of the Holy Spirit gave power to the gospel message and produced in God's people a realization of their spiritual and material responsibility.

THE OPPOSITION TO THE MESSAGE

Evidently one chief purpose of the early chapters of Acts is to show how the power promised by the risen Christ overcame every obstacle. The opposition appeared consecutively from three sources: first from the Sadducees, then from the Pharisees, and finally from the Jewish state presided over by Herod Agrippa I.

(1) The healing of the lame man at the beautiful gate of the Temple (Ac. 3:1ff.) precipitated the *Sadducean persecution*. It thrust the Christian group into prominence right in the Temple courts, which was the stronghold of Sadducean influence.

The religious intensity and devotion which their experience in Christ had generated led the apostles to be rigidly faithful in their religious observances. Their new-found experience presented no reason for discontinuing the familiar practices of their traditional religion, consequently they persisted in the customs taught them from childhood. Hence in conformity with a religious custom of Judaism, at three o'clock in the afternoon Peter and John were visiting the Temple for the hour of prayer. Doubtless the very regularity of their religious practices had been their protection, for the officers and attendants of the Temple had regarded them as merely punctilious Jewish worshippers, though with some rather fanatical notions about the Messiah. There is no doubt they had been discoursing from time to time with the masses in the Temple courts, but their messages would receive only passing attention and scornful comment by the official group. To the officers and teachers of the Jews these occasional haranguers in the Temple courts were but the disappointed followers of the defeated and executed Nazarene, and consequently harmless, though sometimes doubtless rather irritating.

But a startling incident occurred which threw the Temple authorities into turmoil. At the Beautiful Gate, probably the main entrance into the Women's Court, there was daily placed a poor cripple, where he might afford opportunity for the attending worshippers to bestow the alms which their religious scruples required, and at the same time secure material support for himself The Temple authorities were attracted one afternoon by an unusual agitation in Solomon's Porch, the long colonade which ran the length of the eastern side of the Gentiles' Court. Going forward to investigate, they found to their utter amazement the familiar cripple who had been accustomed to beg at the Beautiful Gate clinging to the garments of Peter and John, as he leaped about, shouting in frenzied glee his exultant gratitude at having once more found strength for his withered limbs. The marvel of the event was certain to attract widespread attention, and its miraculous character could not be denied. Thereby the despised disciples of the vanquished Nazarene, whose fanatical Messianic harangues had only provoked their indignant scorn, would elicit from the Temple worshippers respect and interest which might prove hazardous.

Such a development could not be allowed to go unnoticed. The Temple officials took the matter under advisement, and decided upon drastic action. These officials were chiefly Sadducees, and it came to their ears that these fanatics and strange wonder-workers were preaching a resurrection doctrine. To check the pestilent agitation and error a deputation was sent to arrest Peter and John as they discoursed freely with the people in the Temple courts. The opening clause of 4:1, "And as they spake unto the people", means literally, "as they were conversing freely with the people". The populace were asking them questions about the marvel which had just occurred, and the apostles were explaining it as a product of the power of their risen Messiah, probably to the profound interest and gratification of many. Indeed, so powerful was the impression made by this miracle that Luke tells us, as the original Greek signifies, "The number of the men, to say nothing of the women and children, came to be about five thousand" (4:4).

The attempt to suppress the apostolic message was disgracefully abortive (4:5-22). Peter and John defied the authority of the hastily assembled Sanhedrin, and declared their unalterable purpose to continue their activities in the Temple courts. They were dismissed with boastful threats from the Sanhedrists, but at heart the Jewish officials were intimidated, for they feared the reaction of the throngs who had heard the apostles preach with manifest delight, and who had been profoundly impressed with the miracle of healing.

The new movement continued to grow and exhibit greater power until the surrounding towns were attracted by it. Consequently the Sadducean party finally arose in a determined effort to exterminate the annoying heresy (5:17-42). It was the high priest himself who this time led in the opposition. Luke tells us that they "laid hands on the apostles" (5:18), intimating that all the Twelve were now taken into custody and cast into prison. Then a full meeting of the Sanhedrin was called, and the incident would probably have terminated fatally for the apostles had it not been for a series of embarassing frustrations which restrained the irate hand of persecution.

When they sent to the prison it was found that the apostles had escaped during the night, and the disconcerting fact was that though the prisoners were missing the prison was still securely locked. Then while they were parleying about how the jail delivery had occurred, a self-appointed informant came with the irritating news that their prisoners were even then in the Temple court preaching the doctrine the Sanhedrin was bent upon stamping out. There is humorous satire in Luke's quotation of the aggravating report:

"Behold, the men whom ye put in prison are in the Temple standing and teaching the people." The Sanhedrin was deeply incensed at this defiance, but as the apostles were surrounded by an admiring throng they dare not do them any violence, or take them by violent means. It appears that the officers stepped politely up to the apostles and invited them to visit the meeting of the Sanhedrin to talk over a matter of mutual interest. Then when they finally had the apostles once more within their power, and were in the act of making hasty disposition of them, the wise counsel of Gamaliel cast indecision into their midst again.

The final outcome was that the disciples were scourged and liberated, only to return to the Temple courts and resume their propagation of the gospel message.

(2) Thus weakness and indecision marked the the opposition from the Sadducees, but it was far different with the *Pharisaic persecution.* When the Pharisees were finally stirred into action the disciples found themselves confronted by enemies whose ferocity far more seriously jeopardized the new movement than had been the case with the Sadducees. It seems probable that since Pentecost the Pharisees had maintained an attitude of suspicious tolerance toward the Christian movement. It pleased them to see the Sadducees irritated by the disciples' resurrection doctrine, and it furnished them a degree of satisfaction to see their rivals defied by the apostles.

At length, however, the disciples transgressed the limits of Pharisaic toleration. The occasion for the persecution came when Stephen began to preach the Messiahship of Jesus in the synagogues of Jerusalem. So long as the propagation of the gospel message was confined to the Temple courts, the disciples had only to contend with the Sadducees, for in that realm the Sadducees dominated. But when the movement thrust itself into the synagogue, Pharisaic influence was immediately encountered, for the synagogue was the special domain of the Pharisee.

It was therefore Pharisaic displeasure which was incurred when Stephen began to propagate the gospel in the synagogues (6:8-15). The election of the Seven had brought Hellenistic Jews to the front. We have noted that the names of all seven were Greek. The last one mentioned was a Gentile proselyte, converted first to Judaism, then to Christianity. They were selected for the express purpose of seeing that the Grecian Jews received a fair share in the distribution of charity. In this act the church was slowly, though unconsciously, turning its face outward toward its world-wide mission. At least one of the Seven was a man of liberal mind and missionary passion. He turned away from the Temple courts and went into the synagogues of the Hellenistic Jews. We know from their names that the synagogues mentioned belonged to Jews of the Dispersion. Doubtless it was in performance of his regular task of carrying alms to the Hellenistic widows that

JEWISH CHRISTIANITY

Stephen first made contact with these Hellenistic synagogues. Boldly and powerfully he presented to them the message of the gospel. It was met first by scorn, and then by deep resentment. Stephen was arraigned before the Sanhedrin, and a twofold charge submitted against him: (1) that he claimed his Master, Jesus of Nazareth, would destroy the Temple; and (2) that he repudiated the Mosaic code. These indictments were probably distorted and exaggerated misrepresentations of matters really presented in Stephen's preaching.

It was in vain that Stephen sought to defend himself. As in the trial of Jesus, the Sanhedrin, finally lashed into fury by the rage of the Pharisaic accusers, were no longer a judiciary council but an angry mob. Stephen was helpless in their hands. (Cf. Ac. 7:54-8:1.) We must infer from Luke's record that time was not taken to pass formal sentence upon him, but he was dragged in mob violence out of the city. Those who would murder a humble disciple of Jesus must punctiliously avoid defiling the holy city with a martyr's blood. And not only did the Sanhedrin violate their own law, but they ignored Roman law. Under Roman rule they were without prerogative to inflict the death penalty, save in the case of one defiling the Temple. Doubtless they calculated that, should they be challenged on their right in this procedure, they could manufacture a pretext out of the fact that Stephen had said, "Solomon built a house. Howbeit the Most High dwelleth not in houses made with hands" (7:47,48). This statement could be strained into evidence as a veiled threat against the Temple. But since Pilate, who was still governor, was in a precarious situation at this time, and under serious suspicion at Rome, the Sanhedrin knew that there was but very slight danger of any interference from him.

It was the custom for the witnesses in the case to hurl stones first at the victim. In this instance it was a welcome task, for the witnesses were enraged Pharisees whom Stephen had defeated in debate. Doubtless one of those with whom he had debated in the Cilician synagogue (cf. 6:9) was the young rabbi Saul of Tarsus. This irritated young leader, his pride wounded and his convictions disturbed, had volunteered to supervise the stoning of Stephen. But the radiant face of the martyr ceased not to torture the conscience of Saul until his goaded spirit found peace in the forgiving love of Jesus.

Pharisaic passion had been stirred to its depths. A few humble and generous men gave Stephen a respectable burial, but the mob of infuriated persecutors rushed back immediately into the city and fell upon the defenseless church (8:1,2), determined upon its extermination. The leader of this frenzied assault was Saul of Tarsus. His own aching conscience and unsettled convictions lashed him into an uncontrollable fury, which he vented on the helpless Christians. The results were far-reaching. Multitudes of the disciples were

JEWISH CHRISTIANITY

scattered out from Jerusalem into all parts of Judea and Samaria, and even as far as Damascus.

But not all were driven out. That is a pathetic clause at the end of Acts 8:1, "except the apostles". It was too embarrassing for Luke to give any details or explanations. The apostles had preached Christ, and had boldly charged the Sadducean officials with his death, but they had kept themselves well within the limits of Jewish prejudice and custom, and had done nothing to provoke the fury of the Pharisees. In Stephen's death-grapple with Pharisaic bigotry the apostles had mutely looked on, too confused and dazed to offer interference. When the great wave of persecution swept through the church, they quietly retired to their abiding places, and remained in seclusion until the danger was past. We would much prefer to believe that they remained in Jerusalem to champion the cause of the hounded disciples, but it is hardly possible to infer this from Luke's brief statement, "except the apostles". If they had bravely faced the tempest of persecution Luke would have had more to say, and probably another martydom to relate. This noble group made a glorious and inestimable contribution to the spiritual interests of all subsequent generations, and several of them did eventually honor their Lord with a martyr's death, but the disturbance wrought by Stephen among the Pharisees they quietly evaded, probably feeling they had no responsibility in it, but nevertheless leaving a sad blot upon their otherwise illustrious history.

(3) The last great shock of opposition to Jewish Christianity recorded in Acts was the *Herodian persecution* (12:1-23). The Jerusalem church passed through four severe tests in the early years of its history. The first was the economic problem resulting from the entrance into the Christian community of so many who had not in Jerusalem any means of support. The second was the religious persecution inflicted by the Sadducees and Pharisees. The third was the narrow Jewish spirit which precluded any extensive missionary activity, especially among the Gentiles. The fourth was the persecution by Agrippa I, which is recorded in the chapter before us. (Cf. Stifler, *Acts*, p. 104.)

In Luke's simple condensed narrative we find no suggestion of the provocation of Agrippa's persecution. Doubtless the rapid growth of Christianity had caused the new religion to attract his attention, and its Messianic claims had led him to suppose that it was a menace to the peace of his realms. Messianic uprisings on previous occasions had caused serious trouble, and Agrippa could naturally reason that it was better to suppress this movement before it reached a stage of open violence. Of course such would be an utter misunderstanding of the spirit and design of the Christian movement, but it is not strange that Agrippa should fail to understand the new religion. It is probably not correct to assume that James was the only one slain. He is the only one specifically mentioned by

JEWISH CHRISTIANITY

Luke, but others might have suffered martyrdom. Seeing that this persecution of the Christians added to his popularity with the Jews, Herod determined to carry it farther.

Peter was arrested, but since the Feast of Unleavened Bread, initiated by the Passover, was just at hand, an execution at this time would offend rather than please the Jews. Consequently Peter was cast into prison to await the end of the Feast eight days hence. Appreciating his prominence in the Christian circle and fearing an effort to release him by violence, Herod placed in charge of him sixteen soldiers, to take their turn in groups of four at four watches of six hours each.

Consternation prevailed in the church. Verse 5 is quite vivid in the Greek. It literally means, "But prayer with outstretched hands continued to be offered to God by the church for him". The prayer meeting was held in the home of Mary, the mother of John Mark. This is indeed a tender touch which Luke places in this record. By 1 Pt. 5:13 we know that Mark was led to Christ by Peter. How natural that a grateful Christian mother should have offered her home for this prayer meeting! And this was not the only prayer group. Verse 17 indicates that James (the Lord's brother) was leading a prayer meeting in another part of the city. There were probably several other groups, for Luke tells us in verse 5 that prayer was made "of the church", and for any considerable portion of the church at Jerusalem to be engaged in simultaneous prayer would require that they assemble in many groups, for there was no place outside the Temple courts that would accomodate the several thousand members for a single meeting.

True historical interpretation will not seek to delete the supernatural from this chapter. There is no reasonable doubt that Luke considered Peter's release an act of direct divine intervention. Whatever private views one may have of angels and miracles, as a faithful interpreter he must recognize that Luke meant to be recording a miracle here. So marvelous was the deliverance that at first Peter himself thought it to be but a dream. And when the praying group at the home of Mary heard that their prayers had been promptly answered, their faith staggered for the moment. Luke wraps the entire record in the atmosphere of the supernatural. It is an arbitrary interpretation which seeks to deprive it of its original viewpoint. (Cf. David Smith, *Disciple's Commentary*, in loco).

The Herodian persecution was brought to an early close by the death of Agrippa. Josephus relates the manner of his death, and is in substantial accord with Luke. It is interesting that in verse 23 Luke gives both the popular and the professional explanation of Agrippa's deadly disease. He agreed with prevailing Christian tradition that the king's death was

JEWISH CHRISTIANITY 77

an act of divine retribution, but he also knew that the malady with which he was afflicted was cancer, as the language really signifies.

THE PROGRESS OF THE MESSAGE

Acts vi. 7; viii. 4-40; ix. 31-xi. 26; xii. 24

Luke follows quite faithfully the outline given in the promise of Jesus in Acts 1:8 He shows how the message grips first the heart and life of Jerusalem, then passes out into Judea and Samaria, then on out through Galilee and Syria in its irresistable march toward the uttermost parts of the earth.

(1) The record of Acts up to the eigth chapter is a narrative of the propagation of the gospel *in Jerusalem*. A splendid summary of the evangelization of Jerusalem appears in 6:7. The power of the gospel which the disciples proclaimed was ever more and more manifest; the church continued to grow in numbers and influence; and even among the priests, the supreme stratum of Jewish society in Jerusalem, the Christian movement found recruits.

(2) Luke next shows the gospel was preached *in Samaria* (8:4-25). The planting of the kingdom there was by Phillip, one of the Seven. To parley over the question whether Philip's ordination embraced the prerogatives exercised by him here is to import back into the book of Acts questions growing out of nineteen centuries of historical development. Such a

problem never even remotely occurred to the mind of Luke, and hence he offers no word of explanation. An "ordained ministry" was no such distinct official class in Phillip's time as it later became. Philip believed himself led of the Lord in what he did, and that was all the authorization he cared for, and that fact also plainly satisfied the mind of Luke, even though he was accustomed to a slightly more definite official distinction for the ministry.

Philip's activities in Samaria did disturb the mind of the Jerusalem apostles, but not on the question of his proper ordination. The difficulty which they saw in the situation was the fact of a large number of Samaritans being offered all the privileges of the gospel. Even the apostolic group did not yet possess a real missionary vision, and we may be sure their misgivings were aggravated by those Pharisaic Christians of the Jerusalem church who afterward inaugurated the Judaizing movement. A committee of investigation was sent to the scene of Philip's labors. Quite naturally the two leading apostles, Peter and John, were selected for this mission, for the church had entire confidence in their ability and fidelity in coping with the new and startling development. But only one defect could Peter and John find in Philip's work; that, however, a very grave one. So zealous had Phillip been in his evangelistic enterprise that he had neglected the preparation of his converts for a profound and fruitful spiritual life. And doubtless Philip labored under the impression that only an apostle could become the agent for the endument of the Holy Spirit. That such was the divine plan we seriously doubt, but at any rate it seems to have been the prevailing opinion in the church at that time. Even Peter and John apparently shared this belief, for the impression one gains from the record is that they proceeded about the impartation of the Spirit's power as their peculiar prerogative. Whether this restriction in function was divinely purposed or not, God honored the sincerity of their faith and effort. When their hands were laid upon the Samaritan believers the Holy Spirit was bestowed.

The case of Simon Magus is frankly puzzling. The title "magus" simply means that he was a magician, a trickster. By his bewildering tricks he had amazed and deceived the Samaritans for some time. But when he heard the preaching of Philip, accompained by the miracles which the evangelist performed, he was deeply impressed and yielded his heart to the power of the gospel. There is no need for supposing that Simon's conversion was spurious. He did, indeed, offer to buy the Spirit's power from Peter and John, but this was quite a natural reaction of his pagan conceptions, from which he was not yet entirely released. On the other hand, the severity of Peter's rebuke is quite a natural reaction of the keen spiritual sensibilities of the apostle to such a base proposal (cf. verse 21). His expression, "thy heart is not right before God," simply means that Simon was not yet in the possession of a correct spiritual understanding of the things of God. The Greek word rendered "right" signifies to be properly adjusted—literally, "well placed." His heart was not yet properly adjusted in its relation to God. We are disposed to read back into the phrase the modern connotation of the expression, "right with God." Like many a new convert who has come out of a viciously degraded life, Simon was still under the spell of some of his old habits and ideas. His penitent response and ready request for intercessory prayer give evidence of a heart which had been genuinely touched by the gospel. The basic difficulty in accepting Simon's conversion as genuine arises from the interpretation of Peter's rebuke in the light of our own theological conceptions. The point Peter sought to impress was not that he was still eternally lost, but that his attitude and conception in this matter were utterly wrong.

(3) We are next shown how the gospel was carried out *to the borders of Judea* (8:26-40; 9:31-43). That Luke does not follow the exact order of the wording of Acts 1:8 ("and in all Judea and Samaria") indicates that he was not conciously adhering to any rigid outline. In Acts 1:8 he was following the geographical order, while in his narration of the evangelization of these districts he follows the chronological order. It is also a little confusing in an attempt at logical analysis to find the Ethiopian Gentile thrust into the midst of our discussion of the evangelization of Judea, but Luke was following the sequence of

JEWISH CHRISTIANITY 81

Philip's personal experience rather than seeking to present a consistent arrangement of his material. And our analysis is fairly well preserved in the fact that the eunuch was evangelized at Gaza, which was on the border of Judea.

The expression, "the same is desert," refers to Gaza and its vicinity rather than to the road leading there. The ancient city had been deserted long ago, and a new Gaza established near the coast. The principal line of connection between Egypt and the Mesopotamian Valley had formerly passed through the old site of Gaza, but the Romans had laid out a new road by the coast, and a new city of Gaza had been built on the new highway, leaving the original site "desert;" that is, but sparsely populated. It was near the ancient site that Philip probably found the eunuch.

This Ethiopian belonged to a realm to the south of Egypt, where women held the rule. The word Candace was a title and not a proper name, just as Pharaoh for the rulers of Egypt. The eunuch was likely a Gentile "Godfearer" who had been up to Jerusalem to attend a feast—which feast we do not know. As one interested in the Jewish religion he had secured a Greek copy of the Old Testament scriptures, and was reading the fifty-third chapter of Isaiah. No better basis could be found in the Old Testament for preaching the message of Christ. Philip unfolded to him the redemptive truth, with the result that the eunuch received the message and was baptised. Thence Philip continued to scatter the seed of truth on up the Judean coast to Caesarea, where he settled permanently (cf. Ac. 21:8).

Luke's narrative now turns to Peter's missionary activities in the borders of Judea (9:31-43). In 9:31 we have a succinct statement which shows quite clearly the extent to which the gospel propaganda had advanced up to that time. In the three chief provinces of Palestine, Judea, Samaria, and Galilee, Christianity had been established; and Luke's language here is quite likely general in its import, signifying that the entire country of the Jews had been evangelized, including Perea.

Two conditions now specially favored the spread of the gospel. One was that Saul of Tarsus had now been converted to the new faith, and thereby the persecution had lost its most effective and aggressive leadership. The other was that the Jews themselves were menaced by severe persecution at the hands of the Roman emperor Caligula, and would consequently have their attention diverted from the Christians. (Cf. Carver, *Acts*, p. 101.) Taking advantage of this opportunity, Peter sets out upon a tour of evangelization "throughtout all parts" (9:32). As he moved up the coastal plain he found disciples who had already been won by the efforts of Philip, and doubtless many who had been driven out from Jerusalem by persecution. Peter's ministry seems to have chiefly been devoted to the disciples. He was pursuing a "mission of encouragement to the Christian communities which had arisen outside the city." (David Smith, *Disciple's Commentary*, in loco). He came first "to the saints that dwelt at Lydda" (9:32). Here he healed a paralytic who we may judge from the context was a disciple. The news of this miracle reached Joppa, and aroused there an unusual interest, because Peter's miraculous powers were there needed very badly. A noble woman of faith and means, by name Tabitha (Greek, Dorcas), a benevolent soul whose charitable services had ingratiated her with all who knew her, had met an untimely death. Luke here again paints a vivid picture with his Greek imperfect tenses. He describes Dorcas as "full of good works and almsdeeds which she was accustomed to do." When Peter arrived the adoring friends exhibited to him the garments which Dorcas "was making while she was with them:" doubtless clothing for the poor which Dorcas was engaged in making when death unexpectedly overtook her. Peter was called to come without delay to restore to life and her benevolent ministries this beloved disciple. Peter performed the desired miracle, and thereby gave the gospel message a new standing in all the vicinity of Joppa. Having thus established in Joppa a strong influence, Peter remained for a considerable period in order that he might take advantage of the opportunity thus gained.

(4) Finally the gospel reaches out *to the Gentile world* (Ac. 10:1-11:26). Luke gives two instances

of this new and vastly important development, the conversion of the house of Cornelius and the evangelization of Antioch.

i. The ministry of Peter to the house of Cornelius is the first definite effort of Jewish Christianity to give the gospel to the Gentile. And even this effort was not begun upon the initiative of Jewish Christianity. It was initiated by a direct revelation of God to Cornelius. The hand that opened the door of Christ's kingdom to the Gentile was a divine hand. Luke feels very intensely the force of this fact. Four times he introduces into his record the account of the vision of Cornelius (10:3-6, 22, 30-33; 11:13, 14). It is interesting for us to note the successive steps by which the divine hand gradually led Jewish Christianity into the evangelization of the Gentiles.

(*a*) The first subject selected was one who would be least offensive to Jewish sensibilities. The messengers who came to Peter assured him that Cornelius was one "well reported of by all the nation of the Jews" (10:22). He possessed traits which would be especially attractive to the Jew. He was "devout," or, as the Greek word really means, religious. He was a God-fearer; that is, a Gentile who accepted the God of the Jews, read and respected the Old Testament as scripture, and attended the synagogue, though he had never submitted to the ceremonies necessary to make him a full proselyte to the Jewish religion. He gave alms and prayed. These practices would have commended him even to a Pharisee.

(b) Peter was thoroughly prepared for his novel mission. Even his residence in the house of Simon the tanner was a step in that direction, for in the eyes of Jewish law a tanner was unclean. To handle a dead body or any part of a dead body brought upon one ceremonial impurity. A tanner of necessity must handle dead bodies and the skin of dead animals. This he was doing constantly, so could not hope to keep himself ceremonially pure. Hence a tanner would be avoided by a strict Jew. Simon could not maintain his residence among the other Jewish homes of Joppa, but occupied a house by the seaside (verse 6). It was quite a concession on Peter's part when he consented to make Simon's house his home while in Joppa. Luke seems conscious of this, for he stresses the fact that Simon was a tanner (9:43; 10:5).

Peter's chief preparation was by means of a vision. About noon one day he ascended the stairway which went up by the side of Simon's house to the flat roof, on which according to custom there was built a guest chamber—the "upper room." The roof extending out around the room constituted a sort of porch. Upon the roof beside his room Peter was engaged in prayer, when he beheld a vision. A sheet, such as the large awning used for a ship's sail, seemed to be lowered from heaven, swarming with beasts and reptiles of every description. The clean animals were mingled with the unclean. A voice commanded Peter to slay and eat, but even in a state of trance Peter could not forget his Jewish scruples. Never had he knowingly violated the food laws of the Mosaic code. The voice responded, "What God hath cleansed, make not thou common."

The vision had been so timed that very shortly after its appearance the messengers of Cornelius arrived. Peter immediately perceived the connection of the vision with the unusual request, and consented to go.

(c) Simon the tanner agreed to lodge the Gentile messengers in his house for the night (10:23). This concession on the part of his host undoubtedly armed Peter with greater courage for his mission. It "broke the ice," so to speak.

(d) When Peter preached the gospel to the house of Cornelius there came a demonstration parallel to that which had been given at Pentecost. This was convincing to Peter and his six Jewish companions, and they proceeded to baptize the believing Gentiles into the fellowship of Christ's people. By this act these Gentiles became members of Judean Christianity, for no separate Gentile churches as yet had been established.

This act of baptizing the house of Cornelius into the fellowship of Jewish Christianity had not been authorized by the church at Jerusalem. Consequently, when Peter arrived at the capital city he was immediately called in question for his rank innovation and irregularity. The specific charge made was that he had eaten with Gentiles, which involved ceremonial impurity, but Peter detected that this was only the form of the protest—the real objection was to Jews going out and receiving Gentiles into the kingdom. That Peter saw this as the real complaint is implied in his rejoinder, for he makes no direct defence of himself for eating with Gentiles, but cites the outpouring of the Holy Spirit, even as He had been poured out upon the Jerusalem church, as the justification for his act. This reply his accusers could not evade, but it is clear that they considered it a special case, which was not to be repeated until someone received again a very definite revelation from heaven. The reception of Gentiles into the kingdom was not agreed to as a permanent policy, and even Peter was not yet ready to urge it as such.

ii. A much more aggressive and effective step toward the evangelization of the Gentile world was taken in the missionary effort at Antioch (11:19-26). Here without any special vision or specific divine direction, but just as an essential duty involved in their missionary obligation, a group of Jewish Christians began to preach the gospel to the Gentiles. One of the crucial passages in the historical literature of the human race is Acts 11:20, "Who, when they were come to Antioch, spake unto the Greeks also, preaching the

Lord Jesus." Here the tide of gospel propagation fully begins its outward sweep toward the vast expanse of the Gentile world. The individual salvation of every Gentile believer harks back to that sublime moment when a little group of Jewish Christians lifted their voice to proclaim redemption to heathen Antioch.

The effort described in this brief clause resulted in the first real missionary center of Christian history. The Jerusalem church was never missionary, further than, like some present day individual Christians, it gave its consent to missionary endeavor. Missionaries were forced out by persecution, but no general missionary effort was ever fostered by Jerusalem Christianity. It was from Antioch that the mission tides first began to spread. And by its contact with the Graeco-Roman world, its cosmopolitan spirit, and its adjacence to the original sources of Christianity, Antioch was especially fitted to be the door through which the gospel might enter the Gentile world (cf. Stifler, *Acts*, p. 97). It is interesting to notice how the spread of the gospel followed the centers of Hellenistic Jewish life in its northward progress to Antioch. It went first through the Phoenician cities of Tyre and Sidon, where were large Jewish communities; then it touched Cyprus, where large Jewish communities had settled on the coast. From here it pushed on to Antioch, where was one of the largest Jewish settlements outside of Palestine. Past history had unwittingly erected a highway of Jewish life for the approach of the gospel to

JEWISH CHRISTIANITY

the Gentile. And the farther from Jerusalem the gospel proceeded the less restraint it would feel from Jewish prejudice. Furthermore, it was in the hands of Jews with Hellenistic training and sympathies that the gospel effectively broke over its racial bounds.

The Jerusalem church, however, was still highly sensitive on the question of receiving Gentiles into fellowship with Jewish Christians. Probably the objection was not so much to Gentiles being offered the gospel, as to their being accepted on an equal religious footing with the Jews without the ceremonial qualifications which the Jew had secured. When it was understood at Jerusalem that the Christian community at Antioch had established as a standard practice the reception of Gentiles, the church was called in conference and an investigation demanded. It is highly improbable that the chief agitators in the complaint were pleased with the representative chosen by the church to go to Antioch and conduct the inquiry. Barnabas was himself a Hellenistic Jew, and one of broad sympathies. But as we have seen above, he had been conspiciously generous in dispensing charity to the needy Christians in Jerusalem. As a result he had a strong hold upon the affections of the church, and when once suggested for this task would inevitably be the choice of the vast majority. He was the kind of man that could not easily be voted down.

When Barnabas reached Antioch, instead of offering any protest, he entered immediately with enthusiasm into the spirit and activities of the new missionary enterprise. Discerning that an extraordinary opportunity was afforded the gospel in Antioch, his mind turned toward a man whom he had known in past experiences, and had been able to befriend in a special way on a previous occasion. This man was Saul of Tarsus. Being confident of his ability and fitness for the great task at Antioch, Barnabas went to Tarsus and secured his services. This was one of those crucial and sublime hours in human history when a great man and a great situation met. With Paul established in the work at Antioch the gospel message was provided with the means of world conquest.

Having related this victory at Antioch, and the subsequent victory over the persecuting hand of Herod in Jerusalem, Luke enthusiastically summarizes the results in one brief sentence in Acts 12:24, "But the word of God grew and multiplied."

The Content of the Message

The earliest message of the gospel was preserved in two types of tradition. One was the narratives concerning the life of Jesus and the oral repetition of his sayings. The other was the chief discourses of the early apostolic leaders. The former has been abundantly preserved for us in the four Gospels. Only a fragment of the latter has survived in the records of Acts. Doubtless ancient Christian tradition contained many exhortations and teachings of Peter and others which Luke found no occasion to include in his brief history. The treatment of the message contained in Gospel tradition belongs to the distinctive interpretation of the four Gospels. We are concerned here only with the discourses of Acts which belong distinctively to Jewish Christianity. We therefore summarize briefly four discourses of Peter, one of Stephen, and one of James the Lord's brother.

(1) The first is Peter's discourse at Pentecost (Ac. 2:14-40). The occasion of it was the marvelous manifestation of the Holy Spirit's power; consequently, Peter first explains this new and distinctive experience (verses 14-21). He then turns to the ministry and death of Jesus. Clearly his effort is to prove that Jesus is the Messiah of Israel. This he does by first calling attention to the evidences in the known career of Jesus (verses 21-23), and then by showing that the experience of Jesus presents a fulfillment of Messianic prophecies (verses 24-36). Finally, in response to the anxious inquiry of his hearers, he explains how this marvelous power they have seen manifested may be received. If Acts 2:38 is taken as a whole, it may be summarized as follows: Secure salvation by repentance, and manifest publicly the fact of your remission of sins by obeying Christ in baptism, and when you have thus been saved and bowed in obedience to the will of Christ, then you are qualified to receive the enduement of power by the Holy Spirit. It is to be

carefully observed that the question of the convicted multitude to which Peter was replying in Acts 2:38 involved not salvation alone, but also the infilling of the Holy Spirit. Hence Peter's answer means that one should repent and be baptized, and thus present in manifest reality the fact of his remission, to be a fit recipient of the Holy Spirit. To apply this verse exclusively to the terms of salvation is to wrench it out of its context.

(2) Next we come to Peter's discourse in the Temple court (Ac. 3:12-26). The chief purpose of this message is to explain the authority and power of the miracle Peter and John have just performed. Peter first shows that the transmission of Messianic power from Jesus to his disciples comes through faith (verses 12-16), and then shows that this Messianic power is based upon the death of Christ (verses 17, 18). He then dwells upon the authority and ultimate triumph of Jesus as the Messiah, presenting it as an incentive to repentance (verses 19-21) and a fulfillment of prophecy (verses 22-26).

(3) We may next notice Peter's discourse before the Sanhedrin (Ac. 4:8-12). He declares again that the healing of the lame man was through the power of Jesus, "whom God raised from the dead," and that Jesus is the Messiah of prophecy and the hope of salvation.

(4) The discourse of Stephen (Ac. 7:2-53) deals with the history of Israel. He undertakes to

JEWISH CHRISTIANITY

emphasize one vital point. The history of Israel is God's redemptive movement, culminating in Jesus Christ. Jesus as the Messiah has ushered in a kingdom which is spiritual in its nature and universal in its extent.

(5) Of great importance is Peter's discourse in the house of Cornelius (Acts 10:34-43). This is true both by reason of its occasion and its contents. The universal note, first intimated by Stephen (7:49), is here set out with clearness and emphasis. Peter shows that the compass of the Messianic kingdom as established by Jesus is not at all limited by racial distinctions, but only by spiritual qualifications. This truth lies at the foundation of the Christian religion. Peter then proceeds to set out the essential features of the gospel story, which he regards as consisting of the ministry of John the Baptist, the earthly ministry of Jesus, the crucifixion, and the Resurrection. It is rather significant that this furnishes a brief outline of Mark's Gospel, for Mark is reputed to have secured his material largely from Peter's preaching.

(6) We should include here the address of James before the council at Jerusalem (Ac. 15:13-21), and with it the circular letter from the Jerusalem church (Ac. 15:23-29), which was likely also from the hand of James. The address of James deals with the scope of God's redemptive purpose. He shows that God's purpose to save the Gentile is proven by the experience of Peter, the voice of prophecy, and the witness of the Dispersion to the Gentile world. The

circular letter treats of the practical requirements which Jewish Christianity demands of Gentile Christianity. They are exhorted to abstain from that which is essentially immoral, and that which is closely associated with idol worship. Notice that neither requirement is based upon that which is merely ceremonial.

The ideas embraced in these discourses represent many of the fundamental elements of Christian truth. The Messiahship and divine nature of Jesus, the universality and transcendence of his kingdom, the atoning significance of the cross, the divine enduement and guidance of the believer, and other vital doctrines are expressed or impiled in these early apostolic messages. We may see here that the essential basis of Christianity's redemptive truth was held and taught by the original disciples of Jesus. The teaching of Jesus was of necessity the chief source of these ideas, consequently the fundamental basis of Christian doctrine is grounded ultimately on the authority of Jesus.

PART TWO

HELLENISTIC JEWISH CHRISTIANITY

Chapter V

CHRISTIANITY AND THE SYNAGOGUE—
THE EPISTLE OF JAMES

Gentile Christianity should never lose sight of its debt to Judaism. The Christian religion began its history in the land of Judaism, and made its initial contact with the Gentile world through the Jewish Dispersion. We generally think of the Apostle Paul as the sole agency through which the Gentile world received the gospel, but the one from whom we derive that impression, the author of Acts, himself recognizes and intimates numerous points of contact between apostolic Christianity and the Graeco-Roman world which he has not space to describe in detail. His pregnant statement in Ac. 11:19, 20 is fraught with radiant historical suggestiveness. It is a selective reference to a vast development, and calls upon us to suppose much beyond what it particularly specifies. The dispersion of the disciples resulting from the persecution aroused by Stephen was not the only migration of Christian Jews into the Gentile world. Inferential evidence is abundant that many others drifted out from Palestine. And they went to many other places besides Cyprus and Phenecia and Antioch. There is strong reason for believing that they went also to Damascus, Ephesus, Crete and Rome; and likely many other places.

The degree of intensity of their Jewish prejudices divided them into two classes. There were those who carried their Messianic message "to none but unto the Jews only," while others, more liberal in their attitude, "spake unto the Grecians, preaching the Lord Jesus". There was variance in teaching as well as divergence in attitude between these two groups. We may safely believe that the former constituted themselves into exclusively Jewish Christian communities while the latter became a nucleus for Gentile churches. We cannot escape the conviction that by A. D. 50 this development had become general throughout the dispersion.

These early Hellenistic Jewish Christians would begin their propaganda as far as possible at the synagogue (cf. Ac. 18:19, 20). Driven from there, they would continue it in their own distinct Christian communities.

This brief sketch of the beginnings of Hellenistic Jewish Christianity makes it clear that the synagogue and the Dispersion were mighty factors in the beginning of the Christian religion. Together they constituted the foundation of Hellenistic Jewish Christianity, and to them the distinctive Jewish Christian literature of the New Testament is related.

The Influence of the Synagogue

The cradle of Christianity was in juxtaposition to the Jewish synagogue. Just as the thought life of apostolic Christianity was based upon the Jewish theology, so its community life was fashioned after the

Jewish synagogue. This influence began in Palestine, but it is in the Hellenistic world that its results are most clearly to be detected. A wide area of contact with synagogue life is exhibited in the polity and ritual of the apostolic churches, and a literary manifestation of its influence is presented in the Epistle of James.

Practically all the early Jewish Christians had been trained in childhood in the Jewish synagogue, and had been accustomed to attend with more or less regularity its weekly services. It had been the religious institution which held supreme place in their lives, specially in the Dispersion. It is therefore quite natural that it should have exerted a profound influence over the form and methods of Christian worship, and the administration of community life. The connecting link between the Gentile Christian churches aand the Jewish synagogue was Hellenistic Jewish Christianity.

(1) It is a fact too familiar to need extended discussion that Paul built his missionary work around the synagogue. When he undertook the evangelization of a community, he made his first contact with the synagogue, wherever possible. Where he did not begin in this way we generally find reasons to believe there was no synagogue in the community. Such a policy inevitably linked the early Christian churches on very closely to synagogue life. The first converts to the gospel in every community were recruits from the Jewish synagogue: Jews, Gentile proselytes and

God-fearers. Practically every apostolic church developed in the midst of a synagogue environment. Exceptions were rare. This intimate contact with synagogue life in the incipiency of the Christian religion inevitably meant much influence of the synagogue over the formal aspect of church life.

(2) The church developed as a religious community, almost exactly analagous in character and function to the synagogue. The synagogues were independent, self-governing bodies, organized for the purpose of promoting religious life and propagating religious teaching. Evidences are preponderant that the early church was of the same character. Lack of auditorium facilities forced a church in any given locality to be broken up into several congregations, meeting in various homes, but the general character of community life still remained very similar to the synagogue.

(3) The form of service in the churches was clearly patterned after that of the synagogue. Praise, prayer and confession were the chief elements in the service of the church as they were of the synagogue. The services of the church, however, were more spontaneous, with less of fixed ritual than that which was customary in the synagogue. Another difference was that the church placed chief stress upon the element of worship, while the synagogue was primarily an institution of teaching. The Jew regarded the Temple at

Jerusalem as the one rightful place for the worship of Jehovah.

(4) The development of official functions in the church was greatly affected by the synagogue. The office of an elder was almost an exact reproduction of the office which bore the same designation in the synagogue. The elders of the synagogue exercised general supervision over the Jewish community, as did the Christian elders in the church. However, the Jewish elders had no such definite teaching function as did the Christian elders. Instruction in the synagogue was cared for by the rabbis, who might or might not be elders. It is probable that the function of teaching was a development which came after the origin of the Christian elder, probably arising in the Hellenistic world. The synagogue had its "deacons" (Greek, *diakonoi*, servants), but they were not the exact counterpart of the office of deacon in the church. The Christian deacon (*diakonos*) seems to have been a combination of the offices of servant (*diakonos*) and almoner in the synagogue. The synagogue officials were by no means exact proto-types of those in the church, but the influence of the synagogue at this point is beyond question.

(5) The method of receiving new members into the churches was obviously influenced by the synagogue. Any Jew living in a community was by inherent right a member of the synagogue, but Gentiles might become adherents of Judaism by submit-

ting to certain preparatory and initiatory measures. Such Gentiles were known as "proselytes." A proselyte must first renounce his pagan belief's and habits, and prove the sincerity of his desire to become a member of the Jewish synagogue. He was then given a course of instruction in the traditions and scriptures of Israel, was circumcised, and finally baptized as a ceremony of purification. About the only thing omitted from this process by the church was the circumcision. The one desiring to become a member of an apostolic church must renounce his former life of sin and pagan darkness, convince the congregation of the sincerity of his purpose, be instructed in the tradition and scripture of the churches, and finally baptized. The evidences for this plan of procedure in the early churches are indirect and rather remote, but sufficently conclusive.

It is obvious that the synagogue made a vast contribution to the church. Why should it have been otherwise? In the redemptive purpose of God it was the Jew who was designed to serve as the historical medium through which redemption was to be given to mankind. One of the most thoroughly Greek books in the New Testament reports the Savior as saying, "For salvation is from the Jews" (Jn. 4:22). Then there is no need to doubt that the movement of divine providence is behind the extensive influence of the synagogue upon the community life of the early Christians.

THE EPISTLE OF JAMES

In the natural sequence of historical development we are brought here to the Epistle of James, for this epistle indicates more clearly than any other the deep impression of the synagogue upon the early Jewish Christian life. It is written in the tone and form of rabbinic instruction, and reveals that the form and manner of community life and worship were fashioned largely after the pattern presented in the synagogue.

(1) *Character of the Epistle.* As observed above, the Epistle of James is so intensely Jewish in character that some scholars have surmised that as originally composed it was not a Christian product, but a Jewish document, having been adapted to Christian use by a later hand. This theory, however, has been proven untenable. It is distinctively a Jewish Christian document of the first century, written for Jewish Christians in the Hellenistic world. It is distinguished by several typical features of Jewish Christian character.

i. The assemblies of those contemplated by the epistle are referred to by the designation "synagogue" (2:2), while the word *ekklesia* (church) is invariably used in purely Gentile Christianity. In fact, this is the only place in the New Testament where the term synagogue is used for a Christian assembly, thus marking James as the most distinctively Jewish of the New Testament writings. It is to be noted, however, that *ekklesia* is used in 5:14, an indication of the influence of Pauline Christianity upon the Jewish disciples. The community leaders are referred to as elders (5:14) as in the synagogue, rather than bishops, which was a distinctive Gentile Christian term. We should observe though that the Gentile churches also used the term elder for their chief officials.

ii. The Epistle of James reflects synagogue customs more vividly than any other New Testament document. It is the only literary product we have from what we might call "Synagogue Christianity." The situation reflected in 2:2, 3 is characteristically Jewish. The propensity of the Jew toward wealth has been a typical trait through the ages, and it is quite evidently portrayed in the conduct which James condemns in this passage. The synagogue custom of having voluntary comments on the scriptures read seems to have been followed by the readers of this epistle, and abused to the detriment of decorum and religious life (3:1ff.). The epistle itself, with just a few deletions and alternations, could quite appropriately have been a synagogue exhortation or "midrash," delivered by a Jewish rabbi.

iii. The epistle lacks any intimation of the great doctrinal issues which held the interest of Gentile Christianity. The perversion of doctrine is not contemplated by James so much as heresy in teaching, but as a mistake in practical experience. There is but one distinctive error in doctrine discussed in the epistle, and it is a very natural Jewish perversion of a rudimentary Christian teaching (2:14ff.) Opposition to "the gospel" or "the truth" is not within this author's horizon of thought. The ever present problem of the relation of Gentile salvation to Jewish tradition and ritual never even remotely appears in this document. The interest of the epistle is dominantly ethical, just the interest which appears in the Synoptic Gospels, whose ultimate origin was Palestinian Christianity.

iv. James belongs to the gnomic type of Jewish literature, being the only New Testament book which we may place as a whole in this class. The document most similar to James in early Christian literature is that known by the Latin title, *De Doctrina Apostolorum* ("Concerning the Doctrine of the Apostles"), which was composed before the end of the first century, and belongs to distinctively Jewish Christianity. But the intensely Jewish coloring of the *Doctrina* is quite obviously rivalled by James. The literary affinity of these two documents argues for placing them both in the same class as primitive Jewish Christian literature.

(2) *Origin of the Epistle.* A good deal of obscurity surrounds the authorship of this epistle. There is, however, no reason whatever for doubting that a man by the name of James wrote it, as the first verse claims. But which James was he? It is perfectly clear from the evidence found in the book itself that the author was a leader of great influence among the

Jewish Christians. James the son of Zebedee could not have been the author, for he was martyred about A. D. 44, and the epistle must have been written later than that. James the son of Alphaeus, another of the apostles, is a possibility, but there is no definite evidence from any source in his favor. Ancient Christian tradition ascribes the epistle to James the brother of Jesus, the apostolic leader of the Jerusalem church and the most influential figure in Jewish Christianity after A. D. 45. He satisfies the demand of the case better than any known person of the Apostolic Age. If he was the author, the book was of necessity written prior to 62 A. D., the date at which James probably met his death by martyrdom. We would propose as a reasonable date 50-55 A. D.

(3) *Destination of the Epistle.* The epistle was written to Christian Jews of the Dispersion. There is no indication as to where they were located. It is fairly certain that it does not contemplate Christian Jews in general, for it is clearly aimed at a particular situation. The characteristics of the readers which may be inferred from the epistle suggest churches which were wholly or predominantly Jewish. The epistle being written in Greek, we must conclude that its readers were outside Palestine. James says they were "in the Dispersion" (as the Greek of 1:1 literally reads), which expression most naturally contemplates the Jews of Mesopotamia and Syria. Since it is highly improbable that Christianity had gained any hold

JEWISH CHRISTIANITY

among the Jews of Mesopotamia before A. D. 60, we would have to consider this evidence as pointing toward the Jews of Syria. There would be in this region churches predominantly Jewish, and Greek speaking Jews, hence we can most safely conclude that the epistle was written to Jewish Christian congregations in Syria. In fact, we consider the probabilities quite strong that these were the readers addressed.

(4) *Outline of the Epistle.* The epistle of James is difficult of analysis. It is doubtful that James himself had any definite plan in mind. But it seems that some five topics may be distinguished, though without any logical progress connecting them. They are just five more or less independent matters which James had found it necessary or desirable to write about. The question of subdivisions must rest with the arbitrary choice of the interpreter.

Salutation, 1:1.

I. *The Problem of Trials,* 1:2-18.
   1. Trials a means of discipline, 1:2-4.
   2. Need of wisdom in trials, 1:5-8.
   3. Duty to be thankful for trials, 1:9-11.
   4. Character of trials, 1:12-18.

II. *The Nature of True Religion,* 1:19-2:36.
   1. Practice of the word, 1:19-27.
   2. Just dealings with others, 2:1-13.
   3. Demonstration of faith, 2:14-26.

III. *The Responsibility of the Teaching Office,* 3:1-12.
    1. The occasion for the admonition, 3:1, 2.
    2. The reason for the admonition, 3:3-12.
       (1) The potency of the tongue, 3:3-6.
       (2) The perversity of the tongue, 3:7-12.

IV. *A Protest Against Prevalent Evils,* 3:13-5:6.
    1. Strife, 3:13-4:12.
       (1) Resulting from acrimonious controversy, 3:13-18.
       (2) Resulting from selfish human desire, 4:1-10.
       (3) Resulting from censorious gossip, 4:11, 12.
    2. Avarice, 4:13-5:6.
       (1) Futility of avarice, 4:13-17.
       (2) Fruits of avarice, 5:1-6.

V. *An Appeal For Christian Virtues,* 5:7-20.
    1. Patience, 5:7-11.
    2. Pure conversation, 5:12.
    3. Prayer, 5:13-18.
    4. Compassion, 5:19, 20.

SALUTATION

1:1

James adresses himself to the "twelve tribes which are of the Dispersion." So he considered that in the Dispersion there were Jews from all the original twelve tribes of Israel. This Dispersion (Greek, *Dias-*

JEWISH CHRISTIANITY 109

pora) was made up of two classes, those who never returned from the captivity, and those who had left Palestine after the Restoration and migrated into other lands. From his epistle it is clear that James really had in mind those of the Dispersion who had been converted to Christianity. The word rendered "greeting" means literally "rejoice." It is quite a common expression in letter writing of that age, but is found only twice in the New Testament; here, and in the document prepared by the church at Jerusalem as found in Acts 15:23. This parallel is significant, in view of the fact that tradition ascribes this epistle to James the brother of Jesus, and it was likely he who wrote the encyclical sent out from Jerusalem.

THE PROBLEM OF TRIALS
1:2-18

In the Authorized and American Standard Versions we have the word "temptations," but that term does not accurately convey the sense of the Greek word. It may denote temptation, but is broader in its meaning than the English word temptation. It means something that puts one to a test, whether in a good or bad sense. Here it refers to trials or difficulties through which the readers were passing. The precise nature of these trials we do not know. Some commentators think that they were the privations resulting from famine, such as prevailed in Syria and Palestine about 44-48 A. D. Others consider it to have been persecution. The latter view accords best with the contents of the epistle. Doubtless the safest ground is found in the observation of Plumptre that such trials were "true, more or less, of the whole Jewish race, everywhere, but it was specially true of those who being of the Twelve Tribes, also held the faith of the Lord Jesus Christ, and of those most of all who were most within the writer's view" (Commentary on James, *in loco*). Jews everywhere were suffering criticism and oppression, and those who were Christians would suffer not only at the hands of prejudiced Gentiles, but also from their own people who would ostracize or boycott them for following the new faith.

(1) *Trials a Means of Discipline*, 1:2-4. James tells his readers they should count their trials a joy, because of their disciplinary value. They lead to perfection. The word translated "perfect" is from the Greek *teleios*, and means that which has grown to its full maturity, that which has reached its goal or normal end and aim. Looking at the Greek text of verses 3 and 4, we find James admonishing his readers that their trials become a means by which their faith is tested and stability of character accomplished. When this stability of character reaches its highest attainment spiritual growth has achieved maturity.

(2) *The Need of Wisdom in Trials*, 1:5-8. Wisdom, in the light in which it is here considered, has a history back of the New Testament. Beginning with the earliest compositions of the Proverbs there was the development of what is known in Jewish lit-

erary history as "Wisdom Literature." The men who originated these aphoristic sayings were called the "Wise." Their concern was the practical compliance of human conduct with the will of God. All the Wisdom Literature gathers about the general idea of keeping the human life well pleasing to God. Then from the Jewish standpoint wisdom means the ability to make right choices and live as God wants us to live, and to do the right thing under any circumstances. The wisdom writings are dissertations on the practical problems of life. In the Old Testament the book of Proverbs belongs to this class. The Apocrypha contain several books of the wisdom type. In the New Testament the teaching of Jesus and the epistle of James are somewhat of this character.

So when James says that to get wisdom men are to ask of God in faith, he does not mean that we are to pray for increased intelligence. The thing he means to say is that if a man will ask God to show him how to live right God will do so. One who does not receive this wisdom from God is uncertain and undependable.

(3) *The Duty to Be Thankful for Trials,* 1:9-11. Trials bring everybody to the same level. The poor man is to glory in his high estate. So far as material things are concerned a man may be destitute, but his humility raises him to a high estate in the eyes of the Lord. And the rich man if he is brought low—that is, if he loses his wealth he is to rejoice in the sense of the privilege which is his to abandon everything for

Christ, for his riches are transient and uncertain at best.

(4) *The Character of Trials*, 1:12-18. James now comes back to ground quite similar to that treated in verses 2 to 4. There, however, he is looking at trials from the standpoint of their effects, while here he is considering their character. He introduces the paragraph with a typical beatitude. This is a distinct Jewish trait, and marks the primitive character of his writing. It also links the epistle rather closely with the teaching of Jesus. The one enduring trial is to count it a blessing, but the blessing from God is the support of divine grace in the trial and not the trial itself. The trial is one of earth's evils, and may work out damage as well as good. When a trial takes the form of an enticement to wrong (here the word takes on the sense of our word temptation), its source is to be found in man's own depraved nature, which bears its natural fruit in sin and death. Only that which is good comes down fom God, since He is unchangeable in His character. It is His will to bring us forth to lives which will glorify Him. "Firstfruits" (v. 18) is a Jewish figure, derived from the Old Testament, and means the pledge of a fuller and greater harvest.

THE NATURE OF TRUE RELIGION
1:19-2:36

This theme is perhaps general enough to include what James has to say in this section. It is a practical discussion of how one should act as a child of God, the line of thought doubtless being suggested to the author by what he wrote in verse 18. The Greek indicates that this verse has reference to the new birth. God has brought us forth as His children. "Ye know this, my beloved brethren," the writer goes on to say This is a familiar truth to his readers, consequently they should consider seriously the type of ilfe which comports with such an experience. The type of life commensurate with a Christian profession then forms the theme of the passage 1:19-2:36. James shows here that a truly religious life consists in three things.

(1) *The Practice of the Word,* 1:19-27. It is not enough to only know the truth; one should put it into practice. Being a hearer of the word does not suffice; one should follow its admonitions. This is an exceedingly significant exhortation in the light of James' religious environment. The Gentile knew nothing of any essential connection between religion and practical living. The Jew placed far more stress upon knowing the Law than he did upon performing its precepts. He prided himself that he heard the Law read in the synagogue each sabbath, and thought there was virtue in the mere fact of hearing the Law. James presents a vivid picture to his readers when he describes the man who gazes at his image in the mirror of truth, and going back into his daily life utterly disregards the disparity between himself and the ideals contrasting with that reflection. Examples were widely abundant. Two of the chief instances of inconsistency

were gossip and avarice, to which James refers in verses 26 and 27, "If anyone would appear to be religious, while bridling not his own tongue but deceiving his own heart, that man's religion is vain. Religion pure and undefiled in the presence of our God and Father is this: to provide for orphans and widows in their distress, and to keep oneself unspotted from the world." Two chief features of the life of the time were the distressful poverty, especially of widows and orphans, and the prevailing corruption of Graeco-Roman society. True religion must rightly relate itself to these two prevailing conditions.

(2) *Just Dealings with Others*, 2:1-13. It is rather startling to find here a Christian assembly referred to as a synagogue. It is to be reasonably explained only upon the supposition that the epistle was written at the time when Christianity was in a state of transition from a Jewish to a Gentile religion. Just as it is natural for any modern English speaking Christian to refer to any religious assembly as "church," so it was natural for any first century Hellenistic Jew to refer to a religious assembly as a "synagogue." It is quite probable that the earliest Palestinian Christians called their local assemblies by the Aramaic word *edhah*, or *moedh*, or possibly *kenishta*, while the Hellenistic Jewish Christians would naturally call theirs by the Greek word "synagogue." This designation was still being used to some extent when James wrote.

But while the word used is somewhat obscure, the picture presented is quite vivid and typical. Into the Christian assembly walks a man of wealth. Every consideration possible is immediately shown him, and honor extended him from every side. The gold ring on his finger marks him as a man of means, for as such a token the gold ring was used, sometimes several of them. Fawning to the rich was a prevalent trait of the times. James unequivocally condemns it, and describes it as "respect of persons." He regards it as a violation of the command, "Thou shalt love thy neighbor as thyself" (verse 8), and hence one who is guilty of this fault is in the category of a law-breaker.

(3) *The Demonstration of Faith,* 2:14-26. The salient point which James makes in this paragraph is that except faith is accompained and manifested by works it is vain, and cannot secure salvation. On the surface his teaching seems to contradict that of Paul. (Cf. Jas. 2:24 and Rom. 3:28.) But sufficiently close examination removes the apparent conflict.

Two important considerations must govern in the interpretation of this passage.

i. The first is the *situation* in human experience to which it was intended to be applied. James is rebuking unfeeling neglect of those in need. Famine and persecution had left many Jewish Christians destitute. The greedy, selfish spirit which has ever been the shame of Judaism had resulted in the neglect of many such sufferers. James indignantly maintains that those able to help the suffering, and hypocritically evading the duty, prove that their faith is under grave question as to its genuineness. This is wholly different from the situation which occasioned Paul's discussion of the relation between faith and works. In Paul's case a false teaching was abroad which maintained that one must observe ceremonial works in order to salvation. James urges that benevolent works are a proper manifestation of salvation.

ii. Along with this it is important to consider James' distinctive use of *terms*. There are three pivotal terms in the passage, faith, works, and justification. James uses the word faith in two senses in his epistle. He uses it of that trust in God which one exercises in believing He will answer prayer (1:6; 5:15). He also uses it to signify personal allegiance to Christ (1:3;2: 1, 5). It is undoubtedly the latter sense which belongs to the term as employed in this passage. By works James means sympathetic ministration to the needy, as is clear from verses 16 and 17. By justification he means to show a just claim to one's profession, which sense is entirely different from Paul's use of the term. So when Paul says we are justified by faith without works, he means that we obtain right standing with God by committing our souls to His redemptive grace, and not by the merit of certain ceremonial observances. When James says that we are *not* justified by faith without works, he means that we cannot prove our right to a claim of personal allegiance to Christ with-

JEWISH CHRISTIANITY 117

out manifesting a disposition of service and helpfulness. Both present fundamental truths, and they are in no way contradictory.

THE RESPONSIBILITY OF THE TEACHING OFFICE

3:1-12

This topic has no logical connection with what precedes. James must be introducing it simply because there are conditions known to him in the churches which call for these remarks. It appears that too many members of the Christian congregations were seeking an opportunity to teach. Literally rendered, the first clause of verse 1 reads, "Quit so many of you trying to get to be teachers." They were likely continuing the practice of the old Jewish synagogue, that of having the scripture lesson read and calling for volunteers to add words of comment and exhortation. The sense of liberty and privilege generated by their new experience in Christ had caused so many of James' readers to volunteer that it had brought on confusion and jealousy. Members of the congregation were censuring and criticizing one another. This James recognizes as very unbecoming in those who pose as teachers. Hence he calls attention to the fact that the office entails "greater judgment;" that is, weightier responsibility.

The function of teaching is a delicate and weighty responsibility because it touches the most vital point of human experience—the use of the tongue. Oral expression of thought is man's chief means of communication. Therefore, all our human relationships are greatly affected, if not finally determined, by what we say. If, then, one can keep his conversation in perfect harmony with love and righteousness, his will be a practically perfect life.

James presents in his discussion here two facts about the tongue, its potency (verses 3-6) and its perversity (verses 7-12). His observations are made in a figurative form, typical of Jewish literary method.

(1) He uses three commonplace but vivid illustrations in presenting the *potency* of the tongue. (*i*) The bit of a horse's bridle is but a small bar of metal, insignificant in size and strength as compared with the horse; yet with it one may direct the movements of the horse's entire body. Even so the tongue can change the entire course of a life. (*ii*) As the rudder, a frail affair in comparison with the enormous size of the ship and the mighty force of the winds, can guide the vessel wherever the hand of the pilot directs, so the tongue can determine the direction of life. (*iii*) As a single spark of fire can start a great conflagration, so the tongue can originate a train of events that leave sorrow and desolation in their trail.

(2) The *perversity* of the tongue is likewise represented under three figures. (*i*) The great difficulty of restraining its evil tendencies is emphasized by the

observation that, while ferocious beasts and venomous reptiles can be tamed by the hand of man, yet the human will has never been able to conquer the tongue. It may ascend to the noblest heights of expression in the praise and worship of God, and the same tongue can descend to the vile depths of vicious slander. In this its perversity violates even the laws of nature where each element of life produces but its own distinctive kind. This fact James presents by two further illustrations. (*ii*) The same fountain cannot send forth sweet and foul streams. (*iii*) Each plant must yield fruit according to its kind; the fig tree must yield figs, the olive tree olives, and the vine grapes. One could not expect to obtain a fresh draught of water from a salt spring. In view of these instances from nature the writer intends that we shall see how the ungovernable perversity of the tongue causes it to contradict the very laws of the natural world, when the same tongue engages in both blessing and cursing.

A Protest Against Prevalent Evils

3:13-5:6

Again James addresses himself to situations which are known by him to exist. He assumes through the entire passage that there are those who practice the evils he is condemning. Some of the charges he makes are shocking, and seem to be exaggerated, but we must bear in mind that James knew the people to whom he was writing and we do not. There are two prevalent evils which he denounces, strife and avarice, and both were characteristic of Jewish life in the first century. Many of those converted to Christianity had not completely abandoned their old faults

(1) *Strife*, 3:13-4:12. Those to whom James was writing had been exhibiting a harsh and envious spirit. It appears that this bitterness had led in some instances even to bloodshed. The statement in 4:2, "ye kill and covet", is so startling that many editors and commentators, beginning with Erasmus, have urged that the text must be in error here, but the manuscript evidence gives not one single intimation of any mistake. It is simply that extremes of strife existed that are hard for us to realize. But we would urge that this vicious strife was not among the Christians, but between the Christians and the world around them. They had doubtless allowed persecution to engender violent retaliation. Such at least is the situation implied in the causes of strife which are indicated.

i. James observes first that their strife results from *acrimonious controversy* (3:13-18). There were those who were over-confident in their possession of Christian knowledge. It had made them arrogant, and caused them to violently resent the denials of their opponents. In their jealous enthusiasm for the defense of the truth, they had even sought to support it with misrepresentations of the facts in the case, thus lying "against the truth" (vs. 14)—that is, against the best interest of the truth. It is quite easy in acrimonious controversy to resort to conscious fallacies in the effort to entrap an opponent. James insists that this kind of spirit and manner do not manifest true spiritual wisdom. They are products of Satan. Such methods can never secure an understanding of the truth, but will only bring confusion and inconsistency. The true wisdom will prompt one to face opposition without prejudice or resentment, and to present a peaceable demeanor, even if he must confront unjust demands and false criticism.

ii. This strife also arises from *selfish human longings* (4:1-10). The word rendered "pleasures" means sinful gratifications, whose passions rage in the hearts of the readers. It is their desire to share, with the unbridled license of their non-Christian neighbors, the enjoyments of the world about them, that has brought the readers into trouble. Their prayers for relief and deliverance have been unheard because they have been selfish. The conflicts which have resulted from this passionate determination to have their share of worldly enjoyment have led even to bloodshed. These violent measures could most naturally arise as a result of boycott and ostracism. Tumults of this sort occurred in Rome in the latter part of the reign of Claudius between the Christian and anti-Christian Jews, and caused Claudius to banish a number of Christian leaders from the imperial city. Such unseemly conflicts must have been occuring among James' readers. James charges that such conduct amounts to disloyality to God. The word "adulteresses" in verse 4 is used figuratively, and means that the readers have proven unfaithful to their spiritual union with God. If they will accept their unfortunate lot in humility and patience God will draw nigh unto them and sustain them through their trials.

iii. Another cause of the strife had been *censorious gossip* (4:11, 12). The criticism contemplated here seems to have been among the Christians, though the "brother" and "neighbor" spoken of could have been the fellow Jew, who was inflicting the distress. If so, what a high ideal of forgiveness and meekness James is presenting! It is parallel in spirit to the admonitions of his Lord in Mt. 5:38-47. If the James who wrote this was the brother of Jesus, the attitude manifested here, and his reverence for the Jew as such, are in line with the picture of him presented in tradition. To sit in judgment on the conduct of one's fellowman is to usurp a function of the Law, and assume a prerogative which belongs to God alone. Hence one who censures another is out of harmony with the spirit and purpose of the Law.

(2) *Avarice* (4:13-5:6). Here is presented the age-long weakness of the Jew. It was the occasion of censure and distrust in the ancient world; it is the occasion of jest and ridicule in the modern world. It has enabled him to maintain himself against terrific odds in many a difficult situation, but has left a regretable blot upon his name. James' Christian ideals cause him to unequivocally condemn such a spirit. He condemns it by showing its futility and its fruits.

JEWISH CHRISTIANITY   123

i. Our attention is called first to the *futility of avarice* (4:13-17). This passage reflects a very common practice of the entire Graeco-Roman world, Gentile as well as Jew. It was quite common for people to move from one city to another for trade or pleasure. It was a busy and restless age. James warns his readers that this restless quest will avail nothing. Such vain endeavor makes life but a passing mist. The Jew was especially given to this quest for material wealth, and it was more a sin to him than to the Gentile, for with his knowledge of God and the Old Testament revelation he should know better.

This passage is strongly tinged with the sentiment and style of the Old Testament. The opening phrase, "Come now," is not found elsewhere in the New Testament, but does occur twice in the Septuagint rendering of the Old Testament in the very words used here by James (Judges 19:6) (2 Ki. 4:24). The vanity of earthly gain and the brevity of life are also familiar Old Testament ideas.

ii. The author presents, doubtless unconsciously, an example of real logical sequence when he introduces next the *fruits of avarice* (5:1-6). This is a faithful picture of the attitude and conduct of the rich in the Graeco-Roman world of the first century. Arrogance, luxury and oppression were the rule among them. The miserliness reflected here was especially characteristic of the Hellnistic Jew. James here is condemning a well known tendency of his race, but it appears exceedingly doubtful that this paragraph is addressed to the Christian readers of the epistle. It is more likely a diatribe hurled at the oppressors of the Christian Jews. They probably would never see it, since it is unlikely they would ever read the epistle, but James was setting forth a spontaneous expression of his own just indignation, and his words would be a means of encouragement to his readers.

Again we detect quite distinct echoes from the Old Testament, particularly the prophets of that period. The "Lord of Sabaoth" is the familiar Old Testament expression, "Lord of Hosts". It stresses the militant potency of God, His power to punish the defiant.

An Appeal for Christian Virtues

5:8-20

James very appropriately closes his discussion with an exhortation to the practice of Christian ideals. The four greatest of the Christian virtues are mentioned.

(1) *Patience,* 5:7-11. Patience here is urged especially with a view to the Second Coming of Christ. They are to "be content therefore" because justice will be speedily meted out to their oppressors. "Until" in verse 7 is the only reasonable translation. The Greek word necessarily has a temporal force: "up to the time of". That time is not far hence, for "the coming of the Lord is at hand." James believed in the imminence of Christ's Second Coming. It cannot be justly charged that we have here a "mistake" in the New Testament. James is faithfully recording the impression of his own relig-

ious consciousness, and though the actual extent of time was far beyond anything of which he dreamed, it was right for him to be on the watch for his returning Lord. Inspiration must keep within the verdict of Jesus that, "It is not for you to know the times or seasons, which the Father hath set within his own authority" (Ac. 1:7). James could not know how near or distant in time was the Second Coming; he could only express its nearness in his own consciousness—and in that he was honest in his purpose and made no mistake.

There is a vitally interesting historical reflection at the close of the seventh verse, where the writer speaks of "the early and latter rain". These are distinctly climatic phenomena of Palestine, consequently the reference stamps the writer as a Palestinian Jew. This example of the husbandman waiting in patience for the coming of the time of vintage, and of the prophets and patriarchs of old who patiently awaited the fulfillment of their hopes, should challenge the readers to be patient as they await the day when the great Judge, their Messiah, will come to deliver them from the hand of cruel oppression.

(2) *Pure Conversation*, 5:12. This verse produces exactly the thought of Mt. 5:37. Like his divine Master, James urges that conversation be pure and simple. This epistle contains three other close parallels to the Sermon on the Mount, 1:2, 22; 4:14.

(3) *Prayer*, 5:13-18. Three occasions for prayer are suggested. (i) We should pray in time of trial. The

Greek word rendered "suffering" signifies the suffering of hardship rather than pain. It is probably directly connected with the historical occasion of the epistle. (*ii*) We should pray in time of joy. Prayer under these conditions takes the form of singing praise. (*iii*) We should pray in time of sickness. The anointing with oil was a chief medical appliance of the day. What we have here is God with medicine, and not God versus medicine. (Cf. Mk. 6:13; 7:33; 8:23; Jno. 9:6.)

Having presented the threefold occasion of prayer, James now presents the threefold condition of prayer. (*i*) Prayer is to be preceded by confession. This confession is to be made not only to God, but to one another. Of course, in making such mutual confessions common sense is to be observed. There are instances in which confession to one's fellowmen would only augment and aggravate the harm done. (*ii*) Prayer is to be made in sincere earnestness. The sentence which closes verse 16 literally means, "Exceedingly mighty is the supplication of a righteous man when it works intensely." The emphasis is on the working intensely, as indicated by the position of this word at the end of the sentence. (*iii*) Prayer is to be based upon faith. The word faith is not here employed by James, but his citation of the experience of Elijah is clearly to inspire faith.

One might analyze this paragraph by a convenient alliteration by describing it as containing the petitions and predicates of prayer.

(4) *Compassion,* 5:19-20. In this plastic period of Christian development it was not only possible but likely that some should fail to rightly accept and appropriate the truth. Then others might desert the truth under the pressure of persecution. James urges his readers to deal in love with such, knowing that to save them from the consequences of their error means the achievement of a glorious end. James closes his epistle with this compassionate appeal for the erring. His last word is an evangelistic note.

Chapter VI

CHRISTIANITY AND THE DISPERSION—
THE EPISTLES OF PETER AND JUDE

To those who believe in Christianity as a religion of divine origin, the Jewish Dispersion (or Diaspora) is one of the most obvious features of the historical preparation for the gospel. It furnished the most fruitful soil for early Christianity and the most effective means of approach to the Gentile world.

(1) The separation of Hellenistic Judaism—that is, Judaism of the Diaspora—from the center of Jewish life in Palestine lessened the opportunity for a crystallization of the standard Messianic views and other current religious conceptions, and hence made them more susceptible to the new and revolutionary message of the Christian gospel. The constant contact of the Hellenistic Jews with Gentile life had generated a cosmopolitan spirit and sympathetic attitude which were not possible for Palestinian Judaism. The Jews of the Diaspora were therefore less prejudiced toward the universal element of the gospel. Yet they possessed and adhered strictly to the fundamental religious truths of the Old Testament. These facts constituted the Diaspora an exceedingly fruitful field for the Christian religion.

(2) The Christianity of the Dispersion, however, looked back to the mother church at Jerusalem as the ultimate authority on doctrine and polity (cf.

JEWISH CHRISTIANITY 129

Ac. 15:2). This was the natural attitude, for Jerusalem and Judea had been the original fountain-head of Hellenistic Christianity. There were four developments which contributed to the establishment of Christianity in the Gentile world, all of which may be traced back ultimately to Jerusalem.

i. On the day of Pentecost there were in Jerusalem Jews from all parts of the Diaspora. Luke tells us that there were Jews and proselytes ("devout men") from "every nation under heaven" (Ac. 2:5). He then lists the regions represented, naming territorial divisions which extended around the Mediterranean from Cyrene on the north coast of Africa to Rome, and including the island of Crete. Many of these must have been among the three thousand converted under Peter's preaching. Much inferential evidence leads us to believe that some of the converts from Pentecost returned to their various homes, and planted in their native provinces the new religion. Thus the Diaspora became a seed-bed for the gospel, and an abundant harvest came from this planting.

ii. When the Pharisaic persecution drove the disciples out of Jerusalem, they scattered far beyond Palestine. Luke indicates migrations to Damascus (Ac. 9:2) and in the direction of Antioch (Ac. 11:19, 20). It is obvious that Luke is describing the migration of these groups because they have an essential connection with the narrative of Acts, and its distinctive purposes. Undoubtedly there were groups who moved out in many other directions, but which Luke had no reason to mention, and in some instances was not acquainted with. Of course no one would suppose that Luke had posted himself on all the movements of apostolic Christianity.

iii. There would naturally be an intermittent migration of Jewish Christians from time to time, as individual motives or incidental causes actuated them. There is no direct scriptural evidence for such movements, but, in view of the well known restlessness and tendency to travel which prevailed in that day, we cannot do otherwise than suppose that for incidental or personal reasons many Christian disciples left Palestine for various parts of the Roman Empire.

iv. The largest factor in spreading the gospel message to Jews as well as Gentiles was the missionary activity of Paul. He planted the religion of Jesus in all the great centers from the Mesopotamian Valley to Rome, and probably beyond, and his initial contact was always with the synagogue. As far as he was permitted, he pressed the evangelization of the Dispersion. His influence was not a breach with Judean Christianity, but another bond, for Paul was trained in Jerusalem, spent there much of his active ministry as a rabbi, and never escaped from his reverent regard for the holy city of his nation.

(3) The Jerusalem leaders could always speak with a voice of authority to the believers in the Dias-

pora. We have already noted the case of James. About A. D. 63 the Apostle Peter addressed a message of encouragement and comfort to the Jewish Christians in western Asia Minor. Some years later the Jewish Christians of Syria and Cilicia were threatened with the encroachments of a pernicious heresy, which made it necessary that there be addressed to them a message of warning (II Peter). Some years after the death of Peter, Jude, the brother of James, learned that the same churches to which Peter had addressed his second letter had eventually fallen under the blight of the heresy which had threatened them, and wrote, urging upon them some of the same exhortations that Peter had offered.

Thus it may be seen that Palestinian Christianity continued, until toward the end of the first century at least, to exert a great influence over the churches of the Diaspora.

I PETER

There are but two books in our New Testament which bear the name of the Apostle Peter. Considering the large place he held in apostolic life and history, this literary contribution may appear remarkably small. It is likely due to the fact that Peter was not a literary man, prefering rather to look after the interests of his work in person.

In I Peter we find one of the great books of the New Testament. It is noted especially for its eloquence.

Three matters pertaining to it call for an introductory word.

(1) *Occasion.* There is a general similarity of the occasion of I Peter and James. Both were written to encourage in the face of trials and persecution. However, in James the persecution was likely from non-Christian Jews, while in I Peter the persecution is from Gentiles. It is, nevertheless, not persecution by the Roman Empire, for clearly it is without governmental sanction (cf. 2:13-17; 3:13). The pagans were coming to look with growing distrust and jealousy upon the young religion of Christ, realizing that it was making rapid and fatal encroachments upon their religions. The devotees of the pagan worship were, therefore, ready to find every possible occasion to turn the populace against the Christians, or to bring them into suspicion or disrepute with the Roman officials. It is likely that the Jewish Christians suffered more than the Gentile Christians, because anti-Semitism would combine with religious zeal in moving the pagans to persecute the Jews, and their non-Christian kinsmen would join in the assault. Paul was probably at this time in Spain, and unable to cope with the oppressive measures being used against the churches of his founding. This fact may explain why Peter felt it encumbent upon him to address an epistle to churches where Paul had labored. Then there was his apostolic responsibility for and natural interest in Christianity of the Dispersion.

JEWISH CHRISTIANITY

(2) *Date and Place of Composition.* This is one of the knotty problems of New Testament introduction. Especially is the question of place difficult. Historical certainty cannot be attained on either question, but at least we can find the balance of probabilities.

i. As to the matter of *date*, we can arrive at that with great assurance. We observed above that the epistle was written because the readers were suffering from a popular persecution which as yet had no official sanction from Rome. This would place it prior to the Neronian persecution, which began A. D. 64. It reveals sufficiently clear traces of familiarity with Paul's letter to the Ephesians to assure us that the writer had read that epistle. This would place it necessarily later than the composition of Ephesians, which was written about A. D. 62. In the light of these evidences we may with considerable assurance consider the date of I Peter as A. D. 63.

ii. When we turn to the question of *place* of composition we are confronted with a much more difficult problem. Peter sends greetings from the church at "Babylon" in 5:13. This would naturally be thought of as a Babylon on the Euphrates; but there was in the first century another Babylon in Egypt, approximately at the site of the modern Cairo. There would be no reason at all however to suppose that Peter was at the latter place. He might have been at the Mesopotamian Babylon, but this was now little more than a hamlet, the ancient city having been for several centuries a heap of ruins. And there is no trace of a Christian community there until long after New Testament times. Furthermore, it is difficult to explain how Mark and Silas could have happened to be with Peter in Mesopotamian Babylon.

A strong and reliable tradition places the close of Peter's life in Rome. Therefore, by far the least difficult explanation of 5:13 is that Peter is using the name Babylon symbolically for Rome. This view is in harmony with the following facts: (*i*) The Jews in Peter's day often spoke of Rome as "Babylon," probably because the ancient city on the Euphrates had become to them the synonym of heathen oppression. We find it so used in the Sibylline Oracles, 2 Esdras, 2 Baruch and Revelation. (*ii*) It is easy in the light of this view to understand how Peter became associated with Silas and Mark. There is nothing strange in these three Christian leaders having made their way to the center of the Mediterranean world, but it would be hard to understand how they would have assembled in the hamlet by the ruins of far away Babylon. (*iii*) The view is in harmony with tradition. No tradition anywhere, as far as is known to this writer, has ever assigned Peter to the Mesopotamian valley. On the other hand, there is strong testimony from ancient tradition to Peter's residence in Rome near the close of his life, and to his martyrdom there. (*iv*) This view explains better how Peter should know so well the condition of the churches of Asia Minor, for it seems highly improbable that such information would be carried to Babylon.

A thorough canvass of all the evidence affords many reasons for thinking that the epistle was written in Rome, and very slight ones for adopting Babylon.

(3) *Destination.* This is not strictly speaking a general epistle, for, while it is not addressed to a single church or individual, it specifies the several localities for which it was intended. In this respect it is similar to Revelation, which was addressed to seven churches in the same section of the Empire. There is significance to the order in which Peter mentions these localities. "A map of the Roman roads in Asia Minor shows that a letter carrier, making a circular tour and starting from the seaport town Amastris on the Black Sea, after his voyage from Rome, would carry his letter exactly through these provinces in the order in which they stand. Mitchell, *Hebrews and the General Epistles,* p. 232.)

(4) *Outline.* Peter suggests in the two opening verses of his epistle its general theme, for he sets out there the plan of God for the Christian life. The body of the epistle is an elaboration of this plan. So we may state the theme of I Peter as *The Christian Life.* This subject he develops with admirable clearness and logical progress. He first describes in thrilling language the *transcendence* of the Christian's spiritual heritage;

then he urges some of the chief *obligations* of the Christian life; and finally he faces frankly the problem of the Christian's *trials*.

> Salutation, 1:1, 2.
> > (1) The basis of election.
> > (2) The agent of election.
> > (3) The object of election.

I. *The Transcendence of the Christian Life,*
  1. In its nature, 1:3-12.
     (1) Divinely produced, 1:3-5.
     (2) Divinely tested, 1:6-9.
     (3) Divinely revealed, 1:10-12.
  2. In its ideals, 1:13-25.
     (1) Spirituality, 1:13, 14.
     (2) Holiness, 1:15-21.
     (3) Love, 1:22-25.
  3. In its potentialities, 2:1-10.
     (1) The Christian life as growth, 2:1-3.
     (2) The Christian life as a building, 2:4-8.
     (3) The Christian life as a lineage, 2:9, 10.

II. *The Obligations of the Christian Life,* 2:11-3:12.
  1. Civic obligations, 2:11-17.
  2. Domestic obligations, 2:18-3:7.
     (1) As to servants, 2:18-25.
     (2) As to wives, 3:1-6.
     (3) As to husbands, 3:7.
  3. Social obligations, 3:8-12.

III. *The Trials of the Christian Life,* 3:13-5:11.
  1. Encouragement to endure trials, 3:13-4:11.

JEWISH CHRISTIANITY

    (1) Because of the occasion of the suffering, 3:13-17.
    (2) Because of the example of Christ, 3:18-4:6.
    (3) Because of the imminence of the Second Coming, 4:7-11.
  2. Explanation of trials, 4:12-19.
    (1) For discipline, 4:12.
    (2) For fellowship with the suffering of Christ, 4:13-16.
    (3) Inevitable in the course of sin and judgment, 4:17-19.
  3. Proper conduct in the face of trials, 5:1-11.
    (1) On the part of elders, 5:1-4.
    (2) On the part of the younger believers, 5:5.
    (3) On the part of the churches as a whole, 5:6-11.

    Conclusion, 5:12-14.

SALUTATION, 1:1, 2.

Peter addresses his readers as "an apostle of Jesus Christ," doubtless as a reminder of his right and obligation to bring them this message of encouragement. It is the fixed practice of this epistle to use both the name and title of our Lord, "Jesus Christ." Christ is the Greek equivalent of the Hebrew word Messiah, so it is natural that as a Jew Peter would add this title and thereby stress the fact that his Master was the divinely appointed Messiah. This would also be of interest to his Jewish Christian readers.

This salutation contains a succinct definition of a great doctrine—the doctrine of election. The idea of election was deeply imbedded in the Jewish mind of the first century. It finds its roots back in the Old Testament prophecies, and gathered significance throughout the interbiblical period. Especially did it flourish in times of great oppression, such as the persecution by the Syrian kings. Many Jews yielded to the Hellenizing influence, and others deserted Jehovah from fear for personal safety. This accentuated the idea that God had it in His plan at last to save and glorify but a remnant of the race. This conception finds frequent expression in Jewish literature. Through these historical means God was preparing an important feature of revelation, which was to find its real fulfillment in Jesus Christ.

Peter here notes three important facts about the doctrine of election.

(1) The *basis* of election is the foreknowledge of God. God has laid plans ahead, which take care of securing and effecting the election of His chosen remnant. His choice is neither arbitrary nor capricious. He takes into consideration all the conditions and factors involved in the application of election.

(2) The effective *agent* in the application of elective grace is the Holy Spirit. "Sanctification of the Spirit" here means that entire process by which the Holy Spirit separates the life from the power of sin,

cleanses it in the work of regeneration, and devotes it to the purposes of God in consecration.

(3) The *object* of election is service and purity. "Unto obedience" signifies that the design of election is the realization of God's will in the Christian life. The expression "sprinkling of the blood" is based upon the Jewish ceremonies of purification, and indicates that election provides for righteousness in character. Then election is designed to produce a pure life devoted to the will of God.

THE TRANSCENDENCE OF THE CHRISTIAN LIFE
1:3-2:10

Peter presents here for the encouragement of his readers the transcendent values of their spiritual heritage. In the midst of trails and the menace of persecution this was a very effective means of encouragement. The Christian life exhibits its transcendence in three respects.

(1) *In Its Nature,* 1:3-12. One thought clearly prevails throughout this passage; namely, the great salvation which God has bestowed upon the Christian, and the benefits resulting therefrom. This blessing Peter calls "an inheritance incorruptible". He presents three facts relative to the nature of this incorruptible Christian heritage.

i. The Christian heritage is *divinely produced* (1:3-5). God has wrought in us the spiritual change which qualifies us for this inheritance. He has "regenerated us unto a living hope through the resurrection of Jesus Christ from the dead" (v. 3). This idea of regeneration is a Hellenistic trace in I Peter. The terminology and conception come from the Hellenistic world, having been adopted by later Pauline Christianity as a mode of expression for the experience of change which results from faith in Christ. It appears only here (1 Pt. 1:3,23), and in the Pastoral Epistles (Tit. 3:5), and in the Johannine writings (Jno. 3:3ff.; I Jno. 3:9 etc.). A different form of expression is used in the Greek by each of the three writers, but the idea represented is certainly common to all. The form of thought and expression in derived from Graeco-Oriental life; the experience expressed is essential to the religion of Christ. The apostolic leaders did the only wise thing: they employed language and conceptions familiar to those to whom they carried the gospel, that they might establish an effective contact.

The God who prepares the heir also preserves in absolute security the inheritance (v. 4), and guards the souls of the redeemed in order to secure their ultimate reception into this inheritance in its perfection (v. 5). This process is not arbitrary and mechanical, but it is moral and spiritual, for it is all "through faith". The final culmination is a "salvation ready to be revealed at the time of consummation".

The word salvation is used in the New Testament in four senses. (*i*) It is used three times of tem-

JEWISH CHRISTIANITY 141

poral or physical safety. (*ii*) By far the most prevalent use is to embrace the entire process of spiritual deliverance, involved in God's redemptive plan. In this sense it is used twenty-two times. (*iii*) Next to the most prevalent use is the sense in which it is used in the passage before us, I Pt. 1:5. It signifies here the culmination of the processes of grace in eternity. In this sense it is used thirteen times. (*iv*) Four times it is used to signify the initiation of the redemptive experience, comparable to our word "conversion".*

ii. The Christian heritage is *divinely tested* (1:6-9). Peter declares that trials are inevitable in the Christian life, because they are needed for the "testing of faith" (so the Greek). The word we render "testing" ("proof" in the Am. St. Version) means more than an effort to discover character; it means an effort to exhibit character, a demonstration. The discipline of trial is permitted in order that the world may see the results of faith in the unseen Christ, and the proof of love for him.

iii. The Christian heritage is *divinely revealed* through the work of the Holy Spirit as He uses divinely appointed messengers (1:10-12). God has imparted the revelation of salvation through the experience of the prophets, who found in their religious consciousness a

---

*(i) Lu. 1:69; 2 Co. 1:6; Phils. 1:19. (ii) Lu. 1:77; 2:30; 3:6; Jn. 4:22; Ac. 4:12; 13:26,47; 16:17; 28:28; Rom. 1:16; 11:11; Eph. 1:13; 6:17; 2 Thes. 2:13; 2 Tim. 3:15; Heb. 2:3,10; 5:9; 6:9; 1 Pt. 1:9,10; Jude 3. (iii) Rom. 3:11; Phils. 1:28; 2:12; 1 Thes. 5:8,9; 2 Tim. 2:10; Heb.1:14; 9:28; 1 Pt. 1:5; 2 Pt. 3:15; Rev. 7:10; 12:10; 19:1. (iv) Lu. 19:9; Rom. 10:10; 2 Co. 6:2; 7:10.

sense of coming deliverance, and pondered much on what its exact nature and effects should be. The final agent in the hands of the Holy Spirit is the gospel messenger, who has been charged with the propagation of a truth which even the "angels eagerly yearn to investigate" (v. 12). That is, angels envy the Christian messenger the unspeakable joy of witnessing and testifying to the unfolding in revelation and experience of the glorious realities of redemption.

(2) *In Its Ideals*, 1:13-25. These rich spiritual blessings which impart transcendence to the Christian life require certain ideals which are commensurate with their own character. Peter presents three such ideals.

i. The Christian life should be a life of *spirituality* (1:13). The "girding of the loins" is a figure derived from the ancient mode of attire. With a girdle the long garments were gathered up to permit greater freedom of activity. The Christian is to remove all that impedes the progress of his rational faculties toward truthful conclusions in the realities of the spiritual realm. He is to be "perfectly sober" (so Westcott and Hort punctuate), maintaining the poise of faith in the midst of a chaotic world, and setting his hope upon the spiritual values offered in the redemptive revelation of Christ.

ii. The Christian life should be characterized by *holiness* (1:15-21).

JEWISH CHRISTIANITY

(*i*) In verses 15 and 16 we have the standard of holiness. Peter here makes the standard of Christian living exceedingly high. By "he who called you" he means God the Father, for the Father is the One ordinarily regarded in apostolic thought as calling to salvation. So Peter exhorts his readers to be holy as God is holy. If there could be any doubt about the import of verse 15, then verse 16 entirely settles the question, for the words quoted are those of Jehovah Himself (cf. Lev. 11:44). But what less than perfection could Peter propose as a standard for Christian living? It would have been inconcievable for him to exhort his readers to be holy with the exception of a few occasional sins. This would confront us with a divinely inspired admonition to sin. The apostolic standard of right living could not come short of absolute holiness. The probability of anyone attaining that standard is another question.

(*ii*) Verses 17 to 21 mention the motive for holiness. The readers are admonished to conduct themselves in righteousness, "if ye call on him as Father". If God's authority and personal sovereignty are thus recognized in their lives, they should certainly be careful as to how they conduct themselves in His sight. Though a benevolent Father, He is also God of justice. His right to control the life of the believer cannot be questioned because He has ransomed him with the blood of His Son, whose redemptive mission was the plan of God from its origin in past eternity, through his earthly career, death and resurrection, to his present exalted state at the right hand of the Father.

Peter's description of the earthly ministry of Jesus is significant. He speaks of Christ as "having been manifested at the consummation of the times" (v. 20). Our Lord's disciples viewed his earthly ministry as the initiation of the Messianic age. The character of his Messianic kingdom they at first misinterpreted, but the fact of it they never doubted (except, perchance, just after the crucifixion). The Messianic age was the final age, the consummation of the ages, in the Jewish view. Consequently, all matters and events peculiar to that age were described as "at the consummation" (Greek, *epeschatou*). That is, the disciples of Jesus regarded their own era as the final age, and not some period in the far distant future.

iii. The Christian life should manifest a spirit of *love* (1:22-25). Spirituality and purity of life should be accompanied by brotherly love, Peter says. The Greek of verse 22 may be paraphrased thus: "Having attained a proper spiritual condition, and having done your best to bring your lives into accord with God's revelation, seek finally a brotherly love without hypocrisy, an intense love for one another which comes from the depths of the heart."

Spirituality—holiness—love: glorious triad of Christian graces! And love is the climax. Peter grounds this love in the work of regeneration, accomplished through the preaching of the imperishable truth of the gospel. This conception is closely parallel to Johannine thought (cf. I Jno. 5:1,2).

(3) *In Its Potentialities* 2:1-10. Having described the character which is demanded by the transcendent nature of the Christian heritage, Peter next turns to consider the life which is made posible by it. It is described under three figures.

i. The Christian life is viewed as a *growth* (2:1-3). Having eradicated the befouling effects of sin, the Christian is urged to think of himself as a babe, with all the vast possibilities of growth involved in infancy, but bearing in mind that such growth is conditioned upon proper nourishment. The thought of a dwarfed and undeveloped child is sad and sickening. Great is the disappointment of an earthly parent if the blessed infant which comes into the home fails to develop normally. This experience suggests the reaction of our heavenly Father when His child fails to grow. If we are to avoid disappointing the divine expectation in our lives, we must appropriate the food provided to secure our spiritual development. There are two sources of such food. (*i*) We are to "earnestly desire the pure spiritual milk" (v. 2), the food which God prepares for His children, chiefly in the revelation He has given in His word. (*ii*) We must taste of the divine benevolence in our Christian experience (v. 3). Then the two sources of growth and strength for the Christian are (*i*) the study of redemptive truth and (*ii*) Christian experience.

ii. The Christian life is viewed as a *building* (2:4-8). Christ himself is the chief corner stone of this building. Each disciple is a separate stone for the structure. So we may think of Christ as the foundation, and the Christian life as the superstructure built thereon. From this vivid figure we may deduce some practical inferences. The effectiveness of the foundation is necessarily limited by the service of the superstructure; the foundation is adequate to all the requirements of the superstructure; and it is right that the superstructure should be made commensurate with the foundation. Therefore, the Christian life should be made a manifestation of the possibilities which reside in the redemptive work of Christ. This thought is capable of extensive elaboration and application.

iii. The Christian life is viewed as a spiritual *lineage* (2:9,10). The Christian may trace his descent through a divine ancestry, for he is a child of God. Peter is here deriving much of his eloquent language from the Old Testament. It is a sort of "mosaic of O. T. phrases drawn from Isaiah, Exodus, and Hosea, transferring the most honorable predicates of Israel to the Christian church as the true heir of all the divine promises" (Moffatt, *The General Epistles,* p. 117f.). It will be observed that where the familiar phraseology of the King Jame's version reads "a peculiar people", the American Standard renders "a people for God's own possession". A combination of the two would likely come closest to the meaning in the original; "a peculiar possession", a possession in some special sense. The emphatic point of the entire passage is the spiritual transformation which Christ grants to the believing soul. It is one of the focal points of New Testament revelation.

Verse 10 has been used as one of the chief arguments of those who regard this epistle as addressed to Gentile Christians. On the face of it, it seems to favor such a view. But this interpretation throws it entirely out of harmony with 1:1, where the word "Dispersion" so strongly suggests a Jewish audience. Then when we axamine this verse more closely, we discover that Peter is employing language from Hos. 1:10, which was undoubtedly meant for Israel. So the Apostle views this prophecy as finding its fulfillment in Jewish Christianity.

THE OBLIGATIONS OF THE CHRISTIAN LIFE

2:11-3:12

Having treated the basal character of the Christian life as a spiritual inheritance, the writer now turns to the consideration of some of its specific duties. This section of practical exhortation is strikingly comprehensive, for it embraces the three most important aspects of Christian obligation, civic, domestic, and social.

(1) *Civic Obligations*, 2:11-17. Peter here gives a reason for good citizenship which arises out of the occasion of the epistle. It is in order that they may convince the enemies of the cause that the current rumors against the Christians are false. The word here rendered "evil doers" (v. 12), meaning really "mischief makers", was a current epithet used by the pagans in describing the Christians, and was likely very familiar to Peter's readers. The Latin equivalent is used by Suetonius in describing the Christians of Rome in the time of Nero (Life of Nero, xvi). The pagan persecutors of Peter's readers could not resort to violence without the sanction of the Roman authorities. This sanction would be difficult to obtain if the Christians were conducting themselves in an orderly manner. Hence Peter urges them to submit themselves to the legal authorities.

The reflection of the situation is more vivid in the Greek than in the English. The word rendered visitation (v. 12) really suggests a court trial. When the witnesses are called they will of necessity bear testimony to the good deeds of the Christians, "having been eye-witnesses" (so the Greek) of the same. If they have been loyal citizens they can put to silence the "ignorant charges of the foolish men" (v. 15). It is therefore best for them (v. 17) to give due respect to their fellowmen, to live in harmony and fellowship among themselves, to conform to moral standards of conduct, and show proper deference to the Roman government.

JEWISH CHRISTIANITY

(2) *Domestic Obligations,* 2:18-3:7. We find here striking similarity to the practical exhortations of Paul in Colossians and Ephesians. This is used by some critics as an objection to the genuineness of the epistle. They claim that it is unthinkable that Peter should copy after Paul in any such way. This, however, is a wholly arbitrary objection, and one which finds but meagre support among New Testament scholars. This simple coincidence in material would make only a weak corroborative argument, even if there were abundant evidence against the genuineness of the epistle from other sources. The fact toward which it does point is that there came a general quickening of interest in the application of Christian principles to home life at about the time these epistles were written. If we had all the literature which might have been produced in that period we would likely find other writers emphasizing the same practical points. Indeed, among the pagan philosophers and teachers of the day we do find similar instructions. It is not a mere imitation of Paul, for it is found in the very midst of the epistle, while it was Paul's invariable practice to place these hortatory matters at the close. Furthermore, the Greek word used for servant is different from that used by Paul. The only influence Paul had over this passage is the possibility that reading his epistles might have emphasized these practical matters in Peter's thinking.

Three domestic relations are dealt with. They apply to servants, wives, and husbands.

i. Servants (2:18-25) are exhorted to humility and submission even in the face of unjust treatment. The situation of the Christian slave is vividly portrayed in these verses. To be the Christian slave of a pagan master was a difficult place to occupy. Only a moment's reflection will discern the problems which would inevitably arise. Peter's admonition is that the hardships be accepted in becoming Christian meekness and the spirit of Christ.

If Christian slaves are resentful and rebellious, then the consequences which they suffer are deserved; but if they give no real offence and seek no retaliation, then their patient suffering is an honor to their Lord. Their attention is called to the example of Christ, who suffered, not for any offence which he himself had committed, but for the sins of others; just so the slave must suffer at the occasion of his master's sin.

ii. Wives (3:1-6) in like manner are exhorted to submission. In the Greek the same word is used for submission on the part of the wives as that used in verse 18 for submission on the part of servants. This may startle the modern reader. Does Peter mean that a wife is to be as servile in her attitude toward her husband as a slave toward his master? No, his meaning is not quite that blunt and harsh. Even in the case of a slave, Peter would not want him to regard his master as a tyrant. Such is not the Jewish view of the relation between master and slave, and Peter's Christian experience and training had surely softened him even beyond the current Jewish attitude on that question. Even so, as a Jew, and particularly a Christian Jew, Peter would not ask a wife to be an abject slave to her husband. But it is unquestionably true that Peter would expect a wife to be far more subservient to her husband's will than would the average modern Christian.

A much more important point in this passage is the motive Peter urges for the wife subjecting herself to the husband. It may be that in cases where the truth of the gospel fails to appeal to him, the chaste, respectful, considerate conduct of his wife may be the means of winning him to faith in Christ.

The reference to the women's mode of attire was very important in Peter's day. A woman could very easily bring her own name and the cause of Christ into disrepute by gaudy dress. Such apparel was an almost invariable mark of loose living. It prevailed among the rich and those who sought to imitate the fashion and morals of the rich—and the morals of the rich of that day were not worthy of Christian imitation.

iii. Husbands (3:7) are to treat their wives with kindness and respect, remembering that while the woman is his physical inferior she is his equal in the realm of grace. This admonition to the husbands removes much of the seeming offensiveness from the above exhortation to the wives to be in subjection to their husbands.

The final clause of verse seven mystifies the modern reader. How would ill treatment of the wife

152   JEWISH CHRISTIANITY

hinder the husband's prayers? To understand this clause we must recall Peter's Jewish background. His earliest religious training had inculcated the practice of prayers in the home with the family circle. As a Christian he had found no occasion for abandoning this very laudable custom. His Jewish Christian readers in general would continue to observe it. A strained and unpleasant relation between the husband and wife would militate against this helpful practice. The reason is too obvious to need explanation.

(3) *Social Obligations*, 3:8-12. This exhortation applies to their community life as Christians. They are to manifest a Christian spirit in their dealings with one another. This principle Peter enforces with a quotation from the thirty-fourth Psalm. The spirit required in these verses accounts for the tremendous impression made by Christianity on the ancient world.

The Trials of the Christian Life

3:13-5:11

A question may justly be raised here as to whether there is really a transition in thought at verse 13. It appears to be immediately connected with the last clause of the preceeding verse—and the connection in thought is close. The certain punishment of them that "do evil" brought to Peter's mind the sure protection of those who are "zealous of that which is good." Thus the connection between the verses is close, and the American Standard revisers have indicated only a subordinate paragraph. But when we view the epistle as a whole we discover that, while the two verses are closely related in thought, yet there is presented in 3:13-5:11 a matter which composes a distinct feature of the epistle. Hence we must treat this section as a main division. Peter had none of the literary facilities and methods of modern times, and consequently the form of his discussion will not exactly fit into the manner of our literary construction.

(1) *Encouragement to Endure Trials,* 3:13-4:11. We have in this passage three reasons offered for fortitude in the face of persecution.

i. The first reason is the *occasion of the suffering* (3:13-17). If they suffered for evil then there would be reason for despair, but their trials are incurred as a result of their loyalty to the cause of righteousness. Such trial is not only a privilege and an honor, but guarantees triumph in the end: "That, wherein ye are spoken against, they may be put to shame who revile your good manner of life in Christ" (verse 16).

ii. Another reason for fortitude is seen in the *example of Christ* (3:18-4:6). They were not to become disheartened because of suffering at the hands of evil-doers, for that is exactly the experience through which Christ passed. It was the unrighteous who put him to death, and yet in that same death he voluntarily devoted himself to the saving of those who were unrighteous.

The mention of Christ's death brings before the mind of Peter the thought of his Resurrection, and this leads off into a digression embracing four verses. In this digression we find two difficult passages, 3:19 and 20, and 3:21.

The first (3:19, 20) is especially hard to understand. Peter introduces here a current Jewish belief that in someway there would be a divine effort to retrieve the wholesale destruction which attended the flood. This conception took various forms in Jewish literature and tradition, and Peter seems here to be giving it a distinctive Christian form of expression. It is a much debated passage, and many evasive interpretations have been offered for it by profound and sincere scholars, in a devoted effort to take care of the standard views of evangelical Christianity. However, the language appears so obviously connected with the existing background of Jewish thought that its significance is inescapable. The difficulty is, it says so little that it cannot be very well incorporated in a consistent scheme of eschatology. It is too elusive and unsettled to have any considerable effect upon doctrine.

As to 3:21, the simplest interpretation is undoubtedly the correct one. As water became a medium through which God saved certain persons at the time of the flood, so the baptismal waters become a medium whereby God saves people now, not a literal cleansing from sin (the filth of the flesh), but an appropriation (Greek: *an earnest seeking*) of a sense of moral satis-

JEWISH CHRISTIANITY

faction as to our relation to God. Hence by Peter's own statement it becomes clear that he is not here using salvation in that more restricted sense of the cleansing of the soul in regeneration, but in the broader sense of general spiritual well being. That baptism has an important relation to a saved life the whole New Testament teaches. The pivotal word of the passage is that rendered "interrogation" in the Am. St. Version. It means an earnest seeking, or the initiation of a quest after right standing with God.

Returning in 4:1 to the main thought of this section, Peter tells his readers that, in their sufferings, they should adopt the same attitude of submission which Christ manifested, and make their defense through righteous living rather than violent resistance. The great supreme Judge of all will bring their enemies to account.

The language of 4:6 confessedly brings into greater confusion 3:19. It seems that we must say that Peter has reference to the preaching of the gospel to those who are spiritually dead, but this interpretation smacks of evasion. But at least we may say that the theory of another chance at salvation beyond the grave has very slender support when based upon these two difficult and bewildering passages. No such idea can be deduced elsewhere from scripture whithout very strained and fanciful interpretation.

iii. The final incentive to patience which Peter proposes is the *imminence of the Second Coming* (4:7-

11). He but barely mentions the Second Coming here, yet connects it in such way with what follows ("be ye therefore") that it is clearly the motive proposed for the state of life described in the following verses. In anticipation of "the end of all things" they are to behave themselves in sane religious devotion, be lovingly considerate of one another, and faithful to the task in which they are engaged in the forwarding of the kingdom. Such conduct will reflect honor upon their divine Lord, who is worthy of all glory and dominion.

(2) *Explanation of Trials*, 4:12-19. The question would inevitably arise in the hearts of these oppressed believers, why does God permit us so to suffer? Peter offers three answers.

i. It is for *discipline* (4:12). The term rendered "fiery trial" literally means a smelting furnace, used to purify metal. This smelting furnace of persecution through which they were passing was designed "to prove" them: to demonstrate the validity of their Christian experience.

ii. Their sufferings induct them into a state of *fellowship with Christ* (4:13-16). Christ on the cross introduced the principle of suffering into the kingdom, and God requires that all should share that lot with him (cf. Mt. 16:24; Col. 1:24). Peter commends it as a high privilege to suffer as a follower of Christ. The name Christian was taken by Peter from the lips of their enemies. He would have referred to a follower of Christ as a believer, a disciple, or a saint. In sarcastic scorn the pagans designated the believers as Christians. But Peter sees in the epithet a hallowed significance of which he considers they may justly be proud.

iii. Tribulation is inevitable in *the course of sin and judgment* (4:17-19). The world is filled with sin: human life is universally its prey. In the wake of sin there must of necessity follow judgment. Hence a world of sin is inevitably a world of distress. Peter's language, freely rendered, is: "A crisis has arisen in which judgment starts at the house of God; and if it begins with us, what will be the fate of those who spurn the gospel of God? If (on account of the inevitable fruitage of sin) the righteous scarcely be saved, where shall the (deliberately) ungodly and the (impenitent) sinner appear? So then, let those who suffer according to the will of God, by their persistence in well-doing, commit their souls into the hands of a faithful Creator." In this paraphrase from the Greek Peter's meaning is perhaps clearer. The distress of the readers comes in the process of God's inevitable judgment upon a sinful world, and if that judgment begins with the righteous, it is certain that it shall fall with crushing weight upon the ungodly, who have spurned God's offered salvation. Therefore, God's children need have no fear as to their ultimate safety, but should persevere in righteous living.

(3) *Proper Conduct in the Face of Trials,* 5:1-11. Peter realizes that there is a danger of his readers relaxing in their faithfulness in a time of persecution, hence he urges that they proceed in the normal manner in the tasks which are before them.

i. Especially does Peter apply this exhortation to the elders, for the strain on them would, in the nature of the case, be greatest. The passage shows a wonderful spirit. There is a beautiful humility in Peter classing himself with these buffeted, bewildered elders. The admonition he gives them carries the very essence of the correct spirit of leadership. His mention of the "chief Shepherd" points the solemn responsibility of the eldership. Verse 4 indicates that Peter was hopeful that his Lord might return in the lifetime of these elders.

ii. In the first clause of the fifth verse exhortation is given to the younger to be of loyal assistance to the elders in their arduous tasks. Here the term "younger" is contrasted with the etymological significance of the word elder, and not its official import.

iii. From the latter part of the fifth verse through the eleventh the admonition is directed to the readers as a whole. They are to receive their misfortunes with resignation, and not allow the stress of trouble to create ill feeling among them. Peter realizes that the strain of anxiety is calculated to engender irritation and strife among the suffering Christians themselves. Hence they are to lay their anxieties in reliant trust upon God. The readers are given timely warning that this experience of stress and trial affords the devil an unusual opportunity to accomplish his destructive designs.

Conclusion, 5:12-14. Several matters of historical interest appear here. (i) Silas was with Peter, and was in some way associated with him in the production of this epistle. (ii) Peter was in "Babylon." See the introduction to the epistle for a discussion of this reference. (iii) Mark was associated with Peter in some form of service. Tradition says that he was Peter's "interpreter;" that is, he translated into Greek Peter's Aramaic preaching.

II PETER

There are grave problems connected with the authorship of this epistle, but since the traditional authorship is not without rational explanation, and furnishes the best and least confusing hypothesis for the evangelical student, we waive here these historico-critical questions and treat the epistle as the product of the Apostle Peter.

Three other important questions arise relative to its historical setting.

(1) *Destination*. It is hardly to be maintained that this epistle was written to the same group who received the first epistle. Two strong evidences are

against this view. (i) The implied former epistle of 3:1 does not suggest the character of our I Peter. It was a reminder; that is, of the same general nature as II Peter, a message of instruction and correction. I Peter is a message of exhortation and comfort. (ii) It is evident from the general character of I Peter that the Apostle had never been in personal contact with the readers, while in II Peter there is abundant evidence that he had ministered personally to the readers (cf. 1:12, 16; 3:17). But as to just who the readers of this epistle were we can never know with finality. The most likely theory is that they were in Syria and Cilicia, the locality to which James had addressed his epistle. If this is true, then the epistle which Paul wrote to the same churches (cf. 3:15) is now lost. There is nothing necessarily improbable about this however, for there is reason to believe that several epistles of Paul failed to survive.

(2) *Occasion and Purpose.* As is true of many of our New Testament books, this epistle was aimed at a heresy. The author saw a heretical propaganda menacing the churches to which he wrote, and directs to them this warning. The features of this erroneous teaching, as reflected in this epistle, disclose the influence of Gnosticism.

Gnosticism was a sort of religio-philosophy which had permeated the thought of that day, and constituted what we may call the standard intellectualism of the Graeco-Roman world. It arose from an effort to explain man's relation to God and to his environment, representing the age-long grappling of the human mind with the problem of the origin and remedy of evil. Gnosticism sought to solve this problem by a certain theory of the universe. It was both a cosmology and a theology: offering a theory of the origin and nature of the universe which was closely interwoven with a conception of the character and relations of God.

Gnosticism was essentially dualistic. Its major premise was belief in a twofold origin of the universe. Spirit was regarded as having originated from a source which was perfectly good, and matter from a source which was irremediably bad. This irreconcilable dualism extended to all reality. One could escape the bondage of evil only by properly comprehending its place and effects in the *cosmos*, and adjusting himself thereto. The view of redemption in Gnosticism may be described concisely as "salvation by explanation;" that is, salvation by *gnosis*. The term *gnosis* was the Greek word for knowledge or understanding. The adherents of this philosophy claimed to have a higher *gnosis*, or comprehension of God and the universe, and therefore called their method of reasoning Gnosticism.

Gnosticism became a definite factor in Greek thought not later than the second century B. C. It resulted from the confluence of religious and philosophical streams which reached into the far distant past. It was caused to thrive in the Graeco-Roman world by reason of the heart hunger and religious confusion of the time. The human heart of that day was grasping at any development of thought which evinced a disposition to grapple with the problem of evil and offer a theory of salvation. Whether it was the Gnostic philosopher or the Christian apostle, either met the same insistent question from Graeco-Roman society of the first century, "Sir, what must we do to be saved?"

Gnosticism was definitely syncretistic. It blended philosophical and religious elements from many sources. It brought Hellenism under tribute. The Platonic doctrine of the absolute transcendance of the divine and good was used to accentuate the dualism of the Gnostic system. The Pythagorean view of the hopeless evil of all flesh, and the consequent insistence upon asceticism, influenced Gnostic thought at vital points. Then a religious contribution was made from Hellenism by the Orphic theory of the descent of the soul of man to a state of degradation and despair.

Orientalism made an important contribution to the Gnostic theories. From the Oriental world Gnosticism obtained its two basal premises, dualism and mysticism. In Oriental religious thought the universe came from two infinite and hostile powers, one of which created the good and the other created the evil. To the Gnostic this was the proper explanation of the conflict in man's nature and environment.

Judaism contributed an emphasis upon the absolute transcendance of God. For the Jew, especially of the Philonic school, man's only access to God was through angels and the *Logos*. Some of the Gnostic views reflect this influence. The *Logos* idea was also present in Stoicism. An accentuation of the ascetic tendency, which characterized the teaching of some Gnostics, was doubtless derived from Essenism. This would be especially true of Jewish Gnostics.

When this philosophic movement touched Christianity, it found a point of contact in the Christian emphasis upon salvation. The Christian doctrine of redemption appealed to the Gnostic, and the Gnostic intellectualism awed and attracted the Christian. In this way the two movements began to blend at the fringes, as Gnosticism followed its cardinal policy of amalgamation, and laid the very message of the cross under tribute.

The speculative tendency of the Greek mind gathered up these various elements from divers sources and rationalized them into a maze of theory which resulted mainly in bewilderment and confusion, baffling the modern student of history as well as the ancient disciple of philosophy.

Gnosticism could hardly be described as a philosophical system. It was a method of thought and attitude of mind rather than a system of teaching. It was an effort to apply to man's experience with evil a rational explanation. The tendency to rationalize was the chief distinguishing trait of Gnosticism. It was a process of mentaphysical speculation, indifferent to the facts of history or the realities of practical life.

The dualism of Gnosticism gave it a tendency in two opposite directions. Since spirit was essentially good and flesh was essentially evil, some Gnostics, influenced by Essene or Pythagorean views, urged the utter suppression of the flesh with all its desires, that the spirit might thereby have complete control. This produced aceticism. On the other hand, there were other Gnostics who maintained that since the spirit and flesh were hopelessly and irreconcilably at variance, the spirit could not possibly suffer any damage from the flesh; therefore, the flesh should be allowed to indulge itself without moral restraint. This view resulted in antinomianism—the repudiation of all moral law. It was obviously the more popular theory. Consequently, Gnosticism generally led to very corrupt living.

Thus the Gnostics were teaching that which inevitably resulted in the corruption of character and the denial of fundamental Christian doctrines. The apostle writes exhorting the churches to closer application to the principle of the gospel which he had taught them, and to warn them against the false teachers.

(3) *Composition.* We may assume that Peter was at Rome when he wrote this epistle. The reasons for this conclusion have been given in the introduction

to I Peter. It appears that the heresy combatted by the epistle had not yet secured a definite place in the life of the churches, but was threatening them, and so surely encroaching that Peter could not believe otherwise than that it would eventually appear in their midst (cf. 2:1). It is clearly the same heresy which Paul sought to refute in the Prison and Pastoral Epistles. Hence II Peter would be dated later than the Pastoral Epistles. They were written about 64-65. Martyrdom of Peter must have occured not later than A. D. 67. We may therefore place the date of II Peter at A. D. 66. A detailed critical study of this problem reveals baffling difficulties, but since historical and literary criticism are not within the scope of this study we will adopt the position here outlined as the basis assumed for our interpretation of the epistle.

(4) *Outline.* The chapter divisions of II Peter are among the few in the New Testament which coincide with the logical divisions in the thought of the book. Chapter I deals with a true comprehension of Christian knowledge, chapter II pronounces condemnation upon those who are propagating the prevailing error, and chapter III confronts questions which have been raised relative to the Second Coming.

Salutation, 1:1,2.
I. *The Knowledge of Christ,* 1:3-21.
    1. The essential fruits of knowledge, 1:3-11.
        (1) Spiritual transformation, 1:3,4.
        (2) Moral rectitude, 1:5-11.

2. The divine assurance of knowledge, 1:12-21.
   (1) Faithful Christian teaching, 1:12-15.
   (2) The apostolic witness, 1:16-18.
   (3) The prophetic confirmation, 1:19-21.

II. *The False Teachers,* 2:1-22.
   1. Their sure condemnation, 2:1-9.
   2. Their baneful errors, 2:10-22.
      (1) Defiant toward divine authority, 2:10-12.
      (2) Immoral in teaching and practice, 2:13-17.
      (3) Teachings based upon speculative theories, 2:18, 19.
      (4) Professed believers, 2:20-22.

III. *The Second Coming,* 3:1-18.
   1. Mockery of the Second Coming, 3:1-7.
   2. Certainty of the Second Coming, 3:8-13.
   3. Practical application of the Second Coming, 3:14-18a.

   Conclusion, 3:18 b.

Salutation, 1:1, 2. Peter does not give here the identity or location of those to whom he writes, but describes them in the light of their spiritual character. They are sharers in the common Christian faith, which is, "equally precious", as the Greek literally reads. The word faith is used here in the objective sense, referring to the content of orthodox Christian teaching. Peter addresses himself to those who are equal participants with him in the precious truth of Christ's redemption. Righteousness as elsewhere in Peter's epistles, denotes right living. The faith to which Peter and his fellow-Christians held issued in righteousness; the heretical teachers and their followers held to a doctrine which countenanced or encouraged corrupt practices. Peter does not intend his epistle for any such. The correct rendering of the last phrase of verse 1 is, "of our God and Savior, Jesus Christ". The grammatical structure in the original requires this rendering. It constitutes a clear ascription of deity to Christ. The Gnostics contemplated Jesus as Savior, but not as God.

In the second verse Peter introduces the key word of the epistle, *knowledge*. The word in the Greek signifies a knowledge which has arisen from experience. Here it is knowledge which has come from redemptive experience in Christ. It is probable that Peter is here stressing knowledge by experience because the heresy which he was combating moved in the realm of theory and speculation, and knew nothing of a vital experience in Christ. The false teachers had much to say about knowledge, but their's was philosophical knowledge. The matter held such a large place in the doctrinal contentions of the hour that Peter takes it up before he has finished his salutation, and makes it the matter of first attention in his epistle. It may therefore be denoted as the theme of his first main division.

The Knowledge of Christ
1:3-21.

The errors of Gnosticism appear very clearly in

the background of Peter's statements in this division. His effort is to give his readers a correct view of Christian knowledge in its content and application.

(1) *The Essential Fruits of Knowledge*, 1:3-11. There is no break between the salutation and the discussion of his first main point, because the writer's thought dashes immediately to the vital issue of controversy. At two points he challenges the Gnostic contentions.

i. He presents salvation as a result of *spiritual transformation* (1:3,4). The false teachers were likely maintaining that salvation was the product of the *gnosis* (Greek for "knowledge") which they had attained by intellectual advancement. Peter declares that it is derived from "his divine power" (v. 3). It consists of the fulfillment of the promises of God in bestowing upon the believer His divine nature. No better definition of regeneration can be found than these practical words, "partakers of the divine nature, having escaped from the corruption that is in the world by lust" (v. 4).

ii. Peter believes that salvation should issue in *moral rectitude* (1:5-11). In verses 3 and 4 he has presented the internal fruits of Christian knowledge; here he presents the external fruits. They are the Christian graces, and are to be supplied by the believer. The divine nature, imparted in regeneration, finds its normal and necessary expression in the successive virtues of a consistent Christian life. This is the normal result of salvation, for the writer has declared in verse 4 that the partaker of the divine nature has "escaped the corruption that is the world by lust".

The Gnostic theories represented that redemption was exclusively a spiritual process, and therefore the conduct of the natural man was unaffected by it. The life which the typical Gnostic lived is probably in the background of verse 8, while the spiritual result of such error is described in verse 9. Only in such a life as that described in verses 5 to 7 can one have any assurance of salvation, and feel secure as to his abundant entrance into the "eternal kingdom of our Lord and Savior Jesus Christ" (v. 11).

In verse 10 the word rendered "sure" is the Greek term for proof given for a claim on property. So then, "to make your calling and election sure" means to prove the right of your claim to election. The object of this diligent effort at Christian living is not to *obtain* but to *enrich* one's entrance into the kingdom.

(2) *The Divine Assurance of Knowledge*, 1:12-21. In view of his rapidly approaching death Peter wishes to establish his readers in an unwavering confidence in the truth of the Christian message. This he undertakes to do by three means.

i. He reminds them that they have received this knowledge through *faithful Christian teaching* (1:12-15). He himself has persistently instructed them in these matters, and will continue to emphasize them as long as life lasts. And he knows himself to be but reinforcing teaching which they had already received. His one great desire is that they may remain steadfast in this teaching even after he is gone.

ii. The readers are also to find assurance in the *apostolic* witness (1:16-18). Peter assures his readers that the apostles have not been "wandering off after cleverly invented fables" (as doubtless the heritical teachers charged) when they declared unto them the redemptive power and Messianic triumph of their Lord. They have spoken with the authority of eye-witnesses. He then cites his own experience with Christ on the Mount of Transfiguration. In that marvelous incident there was visibly portrayed a type of the power and Second Coming of Christ. Moses was there, who had died and been buried by God Himself (Deut. 34:6). He might well represent those who should be called out of their graves to meet the Lord. Elijah was there, who had been translated without seeing death (2 Ki. 2:11). He might well represent those who should be caught up alive to meet the Lord. Thus was represented an exact replica of the Second Coming as described by Paul in 1 Thes. 4:16,17. And in the light of this interpretation we may understand the words of Jesus, uttered just preceeding the Transfiguration, "There are some of them that stand here who shall in no wise taste of death, till they see the Son of man coming in his kingdom" (Mt. 16:28). Peter, James and John were standing there when these words were spoken, and they all three beheld the type of the Second Coming which was presented in the Transfiguration—they saw the Son of man coming in his kingdom.

iii. The third basis of assurance given by Peter is the *prophetic* confirmation (1:19-21). The "prophetic message" (so literally the Greek) finds a new trustworthiness in the mission and triumph of Christ, like a flickering lamp sending its struggling beam through a region of gloom until the morning star gleams on the horizon and the blush of day appears. The false teachers were doubtless claiming that they had a specially imparted insight into prophesy, and that only those of their particular cult were competent to understand prophesy. Consequently Peter says that the interpretation of prophesy is not a peculiar possession of anyone, for it came not by human process, and is therefore not a mere product of human intelligence, to be discerned by human intelligence, but was written by men who were Spirit-inspired, and is to be interpreted by anyone who can claim the aid of the same Spirit.

THE FALSE TEACHERS

2:1-22

We have in this chapter an indication of how the Apostle felt about the heretics of his day, and also a vivid implication of the pernicious character of their teachings. Peter shows us that they are to suffer a severe penalty, but their errors are such as deserve a severe penalty.

(1) *Their Sure Condemnation*, 2:1-9. History repeats itself. So Peter shows that just as Israel of old was afflicted by imposters who pretended to be God's special representatives, in like manner the believers of his day must be imposed upon by false teachers. But he assures them that without doubt the heretics will receive full punishment for their perversion of truth. He proves this by citing three instances of divine retribution in the past, the casting out of the rebellious angels (v. 3), the flood (v. 5), and the destruction of Sodom and Gomorrah (vs. 6-8).

i. We have in the first example (v. 4) an interesting reflection of an apostolic view of the origin of the devil and his associates. "For if God did not spare angels when they sinned, but consigned them to the dark dungeons of the nether world, to be held for the final Judgment"—such language carries a strong suggestion of the origin of Satan and his hosts, but two considerations bid us be cautious in devising a definite doctrine upon this basis.

(i) The reference is to the apocryphal book of I Enoch (10:4; 54:4, 5), and is not specifically supported by any other canonical scripture. Other passages from the Bible may seem to have a remote connection with truth relative to God's inevitable vindication of His redemptive message. It would be precarious to assume on the basis of inspiration that the Holy Spirit endorses the source of the illustration: we can only be sure that he sanctions the truth illustrated. Peter's point is that if the readers can believe that God would punish beings so exalted and sacred as angels, surely they must recognize the inevitable condemnation of heretical teachers.

On the other hand, we may say this in favor of the passage. It undoubtedly reflects a conception of the apostolic mind, and is the only explanation of the origin of Satan which we can consistently hold to. It has always appealed favorably to Christian faith. Hence we would conclude that we have here a plausible explanation, but should not be dogmatic or contentious in insisting upon it as final. It is unquestionably involved in difficulties.

ii. Peter next deduces an example of punishment from the flood (v. 5). There is no question as to the true Biblical origin of this illustration, but the mode of presentation is as intensely Jewish as the preceding one. Noah was preserved with "seven others." To the Jewish mind there was rich significance in the fact that Noah carried seven souls into the Ark with him, for seven was the most sacred number among the Jews. The seven other persons consisted of "his sons (three in number), and his wife, and his sons' wives" (Gen. 7:7). The description of Noah as a "preacher of righteousness" is likewise a Jewish conception, though correctly deduced from the inspired record. It has "no verbal counterpart in the language of the Old Testament, but it is obviously implied in the substance of the narrative" (Plumtre, *The Cambridge Bible*, in loco).

iii. A fitting climax in this series of examples is the horrible fate of Sodom and Gomorrah (2:6-8). "A punishment by fire follows a punishment by water" (Moffat, *The General Epistles,* page 194). The charitable description of Lot (vs. 7, 8) is for no reason to be regarded as incorrect, though it is based upon Jewish tradition rather than a definite Old Testament record.

In verse 9 a converse application is derived from the case of Noah and Lot. "The Lord knows how to rescue the godly from trials, while he holds the unrighteous in a state of punishment unto the day of judgment." This is for the encouragement of the loyal members of the churches. Though divine retribution is to fall upon the propagandists of error, the faithful shall be preserved from harm.

(2) *Their Baneful Errors,* 2:10-22. In his pronouncement of condemnation upon the false teachers, Peter turns to a discussion of their character and teachings. This passage is of great historical interest. We get here some valuable hints as to the nature and effects of the heresy which was threatening the readers. Several of its chief features may be discerned.

i. They were defiant toward divine beings (2:10-12). It is likely that the errorists did not deny the existence of angels, nor defy divine authority as such, but in their speculative cosmology they utilized the angelic creation in such way as to be regarded by Peter as blasphemy. The word rendered "railing" in this passage meant defiant disregard of divine character. Peter believed that the wild fancies of Gnosticism had reflected insult upon the sacred order of the angels, and therefore constituted blasphemy.

ii. They were guilty of *immoral* teaching and practice (2:13-17). It appears that they condoned such forms of corruption as arise directly from indulgence of physical cravings, such as revelling, adultery and covetousness. Such a policy is an obviously easy conclusion derived from extreme dualism.

iii. They based their teachings upon *speculative* theories (2:18, 19). This seems to be the import of "uttering great swelling words of vanity" (v. 18). By these theories they sought to prove a liberty which led to extreme forms of corruption. This also sounds very much like some results of the dualistic views of Gnosticism.

iv. The false teachers had been *professed Christians* (2:20-22). They had heard the Christian message, and for a time had lived in the light of its moral and spiritual ideals. But the transformation had not been sufficiently radical: the old nature revived and dominated again. It was like the dog returning to his own vomit, the dog nature assuming control. They had not undergone a radical transformation but were like the sow that is washed clean outwardly, but inwardly still remains a sow: inevitably she will go back to her wallowing in the mire. To go any deeper in interpreting the facts of their experience we would need to call in all the light of the New Testament on these matters, and not settle the question by this passage alone. Peter's point is that they had once been in line with the truth and had now repudiated it. The problem of whether they had ever been saved or not is not within the horizon of his thought. It is only the evident fact that the truth had never taken sufficiently vital hold upon them that he is concerned about, and seeks to represent in the figure of the dog and the hog.

The Second Coming

3:1-18a

Whether we have before us here the same heretical teachers contemplated in the second chapter we cannot tell. It may be that pagan scoffers are confuted here. At any rate, ridicule is being thrust at Peter's readers because the Lord tarries his second advent.

(1) *Mockery of the Second Coming*, 3:1-7. Peter here, as in former epistle, calls attention to the exhortation of prophecy, and of Christ through the apostles, to be on the alert and watchful for the Second Coming. For two reasons we cannot regard

this as a reference to I Peter. (*i*) We do not believe I Peter was written to the same churches as this epistle. (*ii*) The only reference in I Peter to the Second Coming is 4:7, and the sense of that passage does not even approximate the ideas expressed here. We therefore conclude that the reference is to some writing now lost.

Peter assures his readers that they are to meet ridicule, but this very ridicule is one evidence that the kingdom of God is in its final period of development. This mockery is based upon an inadequate conception of the power and wisdom of God. His plan is laid out and the present sinful order is doomed, but it awaits the time appointed in the infinite purpose of God.

(2) *Certainity of the Second Coming,* 3:8-13. The certainty of the Second Coming is here explained from two points of view. The first is the Lord's disregard of the matter of time, and His subordination of it to the higher interests of human destiny (vs. 8, 9). The second is the certainty that God has a plan for the consummation of His universe (vs. 10-13). Peter's language here is distinctly apocalyptic in character, and we should be cautious how we take it as rigidly literal prophesy. It is meant to indicate the divine purpose that the present order shall not stand forever, and should not be construed as a cosmological program for the end of time.

(3) *Practical Application of the Second Coming*, 3:14-18a. Peter views the Second Coming of Christ as a great Christian incentive. If the believer properly contemplates this glorious consummation, certain facts should follow in his life.

i. It should be an incentive to *holy living* (v.14). The proper state for the Christian in the light of this great event is harmony and fellowship with other believers and unimpeachable purity of life. Peter would have thought it very inconsistent with the significance of this great event for Christians to engage in strife over it, censuring and vilifying one another, and presenting conduct which would bring reproach upon the truth of Christ.

ii. It should be an incentive to *evangelistic diligence* (vs. 15, 16). The believer should "account that the long suffering of our Lord is salvation". He should realize that the delay of the Lord's return is but the prolongation of the opportunity to bring men to repentance. Peter considers that Paul so construed it.

iii. It should be an incentive to *loyalty to the truth* (vs. 17, 18). Let the believer beware that the Lord's coming may not find him an advocate of error which is hurtful to the progress of his kingdom. On the other hand, he should seek to develop in both Christian character and Christian culture: "in the grace and knowledge of our Lord and Savior Jesus Christ."

CONCLUSION, 3:18b

Peter closes his epistle with a simple benediction. Such seems to have obtained as a customary form in Christian writings of this time. Paul adhered to it from the beginning, but we cannot say whether he originated it. No such benediction is found at the close of the epistle of James, the only New Testament document which is entirely independent of Pauline influence. So we may at least say that as far as we have any evidence Paul established the custom of closing Christian epistles with a benediction.

JUDE

We have before us here one of the shortest of the New Testament epistles. It compares in this respect with Philemon and II and III John, all of which have but one chapter. These little documents must have been exceedingly precious to their first recipients, to have been preserved for future generations when undoubtedly a vast abundance of similar documents perished. We have here an evidence of the divine interest in our New Testament canon.

(1) *Composition.* We probably have here another epistle from the hand of a half-brother of our Lord. The salutation designates the author as, "Jude, a servant of Jesus Christ, also a brother of James" (verse 1). Christian tradition has generally regarded the James here referred to as the brother of our Lord by that name, the apostolic leader of Judean Christianity. If

we seek definite identity as to author, no better hypothesis can be secured than this tradition. However, this tradition is very late, and is confused by variations and other contradictory traditions. So the only thing of which we can be positive about the author is that it was writen by an influential Christian leader named Jude. Probabilities strongly favor the supposition that he was a Jewish Christian.

The most probable guess we can make at the place of composition is to name Jerusalem. Yet we know that Jude the brother of James extended rather widely his apostolic labors (cf. 1 Co. 9:5), so if he wrote it we can only suggest Jerusalem as a possibility.

The date likewise is in the realm of conjecture. The relation of the epistle to II Peter would suggest as the date A. D. 70 to 75.

(2) *Destination.* The readers were most probably those with whom Jude had come in contact in missionary activities (cf. 1 Co. 9:5). We may suppose that he was associated to a considerable extent with Peter in missionary labors, and in consequence of this fact he bears a relationship which occasions him to write to the same churches to which Peter had addressed a letter a few years before. That is, the readers are likely the same as those to whom II Peter was addressed. We have above expressed our opinion that these were Christian Jews, perhaps Hellenistic Jewish Christian congregations, in Syria and Cilicia.

(3) *Occasion and Purpose.* The churches addressed had been invaded by heretics who lived profligate lives, but boasted of their possession of superior knowledge. One immediately detects Gnostic characteristics in these traits. Jude writes to condem these heretics and instruct the churches how to conduct themselves in relation to the disturbance.

(4) *Relation to II Peter.* A comparison of this epistle with the second chapter of II Peter will reveal that much of the material of the latter is contained in Jude. We have observed that Jude was probably writing to the same churches relative to the same heresy. Consequently he drew on Peter for forceful and applicable material which was already at hand, and with which the readers were already familiar. It was Jude's way of saying, "Remember what the aged apostle said to you" (cf. v. 17). If Jude had labored with Peter in these churches, he knew just how impressive it would be to remind them what the old apostle had written them. We also note that Jude was forced by an emergency to write rather hastily and unexpectedly, and would under such circumstances welcome aid which was ready to hand in Peter's second epistle. The heretical encroachments which threatened the churches when Peter wrote, are now an accomplished condition in their very midst, with teachers and followers constituting a distinct faction.

(5) *Outline.* This brief epistle is subject to a clear and definite analysis. Its parts stand out distinct-

ly. The writer begins with a typical salutation, and a brief word about the occasion which has inspired him to write. He then takes up the heresy, first warning of the inevitable doom of those who thus oppose God's truth. He then adds a word of exhortation to those who have remained loyal, and concludes with a beautiful benediction. On the basis of this analysis we offer the following outline:

Introduction, 1-4.

(1) Salutation, 1, 2.
(2) Occasion of the epistle, 3, 4.

I. *Condemnation of the Heretics,* 5-16.
   1. Proofs of their condemnation, 5-7.
      (1) The experience of Israel, 5.
      (2) The fate of the rebellious angels, 6.
      (3) The destruction of Sodom and Gomorrah, 7.
   2. Reasons for their condemnation, 8-16.
      (1) Their propagation of error, 8-11.
      (2) Their impure conduct, 12-16.

II. *Exhortation of the Faithful,* 17-23.
   1. The apostolic warning, 17-19.
   2. The correct attitude toward error, 20-23.

Conclusion, 24, 25.

The justification of this analysis will appear more clearly as we proceed with the exposition of this intensely interesting little document.

Introduction

Verses 1-4

One is reminded here of Paul, so many of whose epistles begin with a rather distinct introduction; but upon close observation we discover that the likeness is more in the expositor's form of outlining than in similarity of composition between the two writers. Jude begins with the famaliar salutation, common to all letter writing of the period, and a brief explanation of how he came to write this brief message.

(1) *Salutation*, 1, 2. This salutation is in some degree distinctive, though bearing considerable similarity to those of Peter and James. Jude was very naturally influenced in thought and expression by these two great Christian leaders. He designates himself only as "a bondservant of Jesus Christ, also a brother of James." We have no way of knowing from this epistle what James it is to whom he refers, so we can do no better than rely on early Christian tradition, which designates him as the brother of Jesus.

Jude affords us likewise no definite clue as to those to whom the epistle is addressed. He describes them in terms of their spiritual qualities. Two such qualities characterize them. They are "the redeemed who are beloved by God and kept by Jesus Christ." The word rendered "called" in our English version signifies God's effective operation in redeeming the soul of the believer. It is not a passive call, but an active and effective call. We therefore render it "the redeemed," as more closely approximating its full meaning than the English expression "the called."

(2) *Occasion of the Epistle*, 3, 4. Jude begins by saying, "Beloved, while executing all diligence to write unto you concerning our mutual salvation, I have suddenly found it necessary to urge you to aggressively contend for the faith once for all delivered to the saints" (v. 3). He was diligently applying himself to the task of preparing an elaborate epistle on the subject of "Our Mutual Salvation," when the disconcerting news reached him that some heretical teachers had invaded the very group of churches to which he was intending to forward his extended treatise. Consequently, he must defer the larger task, and hasten to them this short but very pointed and severe message of correction. In the pressure of the circumstances and his own desire to get back to what he regards as his larger and more important task, he expedites his effort by using material from a message of warning and reproof which the apostle Peter had addressed to them several years before. This would save time, and probably be more effective than for Jude to send them a purely original message on these disputed issues. Whether he ever completed the larger treatise we do not know; at least it never came to have wide circulation, for no trace of it remains in early Christian literature or tradition, and a lengthy and well wrought treatise by Jude the brother of the Lord,

if used to any extent, would have left its impression somewhere; and this reference by the author is the only trace we have of it.

Verse 4 describes the approach of the false teachers. "For certain persons have crept in by stealth, who were long ago foreordained to condemnation, devoid of right relation to God, changing the grace of our God into an excuse for immorality, and denying our only Master and Lord, Jesus Christ." The Gnostic propagandists had been shrewd and seductive in their approach. The Greek literally rendered means, "have slipped in around the edges." Jude does not regard them as genuine Christians, but as already under divine condemnation, having failed of right relation to God and abused the privileges of grace, repudiating the true interpretation of Christ. To warn his readers against these propagandists of error is Jude's reason for writing the epistle. He first pronounces condemnation upon the heretics, then offers an exhortation to the faithful.

CONDEMNATION OF THE HERETICS
Verses 5 to 16

The plan here is very much like that found in the second chapter of II Peter, since the material is taken largely from that source. The facts reflected are also parallel to those found in II Peter.

(1) *Proofs of Their Condemnation*, 5-7. That such propagandists will meet the just judgment of God,

Jude cannot doubt. He regards the past as offering its own solemn testimony to the inevitable certainty of their doom. There are three of these witnesses from past history.

i. There is the experience of Israel (v. 5). "Now I wish to remind you," Jude says, "you who have been thoroughly instructed." The Greek word here rendered "know" in our common English versions, is the word which means to know as a result of information or instruction. Jude knew the readers had been thoroughly instructed—doubtless he himself had had some part in teaching them.

At one point in verse 5 the original text is seriously confused. Where our English version reads, "that the Lord, having saved a people out of the land of Egypt," many of the best ancient manuscripts read "that Jesus, etc." That is, the Greek word used is the word generally rendered Jesus. But it really means Joshua, which was the Hebrew name of our Lord. We believe that here it is the correct text, and refers to Joshua, the successor of Moses. The impressive example of retribution which Jude has in mind is the destruction of faithless Achan and his household for his treason at Ai (Josh. 7:1ff.). We would render the passage thus: "that Joshua, having saved a people from the land of Egypt, afterward destroyed those who did not believe." If this is the correct reading, then it looks upon the work of Joshua as the effective culmination of the escape from Egypt, and his punishment of Achan as an administration of divine justice for disloyalty to God's commandments.

ii. Then there was the fate of the rebellious angels (v. 6). In spite of their superior estate, they were forced to leave "the dwelling-place to which they were adapted," and are kept "in eternal bonds under darkness, awaiting that great day of final judgment." This is a vivid reflection of ideas, and even bears strong similarity to language of the Jewish apocalypse known as I Enoch. However, it was standard traditional theology of Judaism in Jude's day; consequently, we cannot be sure he is alluding to the apocryphal book. At any rate, whatever be the source of the reference, it is used here only as an illustration, and not as a teaching of revealed truth concerning the universe. We should no more regard the Holy Spirit as here endorsing traditional Jewish angelology, than we would regard our Lord as endorsing the conduct of the unjust steward in the parable recorded in Luke 16:1ff. In both instances we are dealing with an illustration, and revelation indorses the truth illustrated and not every detail and aspect of the illustration. So whether Jude secured this illustration from I Enoch or not need not disturb us: the truth he enforces is perfectly valid; that God will surely vindicate His righteousness.

iii. Furthermore, Sodom and Gommorrah, by reason of their unrestrained wickedness, were destroyed, and thereby became an example of the manner in which God's wrath would be visited upon incorrigible opposition to His will (v. 7). Jude's description of the inhabitants of these doomed cities as "practicing fornication without restraint and going away after other flesh" is probably an allusion to the debauchery resulting in some instances from Gnostic teachings. Sodom and Gomorrah were specially adaptable to Jude's purposes because of the extreme sensuality of their wickedness, which was analogous to conditions resulting from Gnostic antinomianism.

Note the progress of Jude's verdict of condemnation in these verses. In verse 5 the offenders are described as having been "destroyed," in verse 6 as being kept "in eternal bonds under darkness, awaiting that great day of final judgment," and in verse 7 as "having been subjected to the punishment of eternal fire."

(2) *Reasons For Their Condemnation,* 8-16. Jude would next show the unquestionable justice of the condemnation of these false teachers.

i. The first reason is seen in their *propagation of error* (8-11). "And besides, in like manner, these false teachers, by reason of their theoretical speculations, indulge in sensual practices, lightly scorn the higher powers, and blaspheme divine beings" (v. 8). This language vividly portrays the characteristic traits of Gnosticism, with its vague metaphysical systems, its repudiation of moral restraint, and its free handling of the realm of angelology, so sacred to the

JEWISH CHRISTIANITY 189

Jew. The philosophical juggling of angelic orders in the Gnostic theories was nothing less than deliberate blasphemy to Jude, with his intense Jewish sensibilities. And in taking such blasphemous liberties with the higher realms of being they assume a prerogative which even an archangel declined to exercise. In accordance with a tradition familiar to Jude's readers, when Michael once contended with Satan over the body of Moses, even though Satan accused Moses of having committed murder when he slew the Egyptian, and as therefore being his rightful property, the archangel "did not dare to assail him with scornful judgment," but observed the great principle of divine retribution revealed in Zech. 3:2, and merely said, "The Lord shall rebuke thee." This was especially impressive to Jewish readers, for in Jewish tradition Michael was the angelic champion of Israel.

Very different was the attitude manifested by these Gnostic heretics. "But on the contrary, these rail in scorn at things about which they know nothing, then what by physical instinct as dumb brutes they do understand, by these they are destroyed" (v. 10). They devised vain and irreverent philosophies about the sacred realities of the spiritual world, blundering on in hopeless error, granting unlimited indulgence to their physical apetites and thereby accomplishing their own moral and spiritual ruin. Like Cain, they harbor hatred in their hearts; like Balaam, they are the slaves of lust and avarice; like Korah, they are promoters of dissension and schism. These traits were prominently characteristic of the Gnostics.

ii. These heretics also stand condemned by their *impure conduct* (12-16). Several intimations have already been given of this trait, but in these verses Jude sweeps out in a tirade of denunciation which, though undoubtedly deserved, is scathingly severe. The current English versions have softened his language somewhat. The Greek is terrific. It may be freely rendered thus: "These are treachrous reefs as they participate with you in your love feasts, presumptuously acting as providers of charity to themselves; clouds wind-hurtled and waterless; trees which have withered away without bearing fruit, doubly dead, rooted up; wild sea-waves, frothing forth their own shame; vagabond stars, for whom the blackness of darkness has been kept forever. Now also with reference to these Enoch, seventh from Adam, prophesied saying, 'Behold the Lord came in the midst of His holy myriads to execute judgment upon all, and to convict all the impious of all the impious deeds which they have committed in their impious pursuits, and of all the violent things which impious sinners have said against Him.' These are murmurers, complainers, proceeding according to their own desires, and their mouth speaks arrogantly, flattering vain exhibitions of pride for the sake of personal profit."

The love feasts of the early Christian afforded the Gnostics a wide opportunity for perversion and

JEWISH CHRISTIANITY 191

corruption. They were usually held following the Lord's Supper, and were fellowship occasions in which the church or some of its wealthy members provided a feast. The dissoluteness of the Gnostic furnished encouragement to gluttony and unchaste conduct on these occasions. The food was given free, and the false teachers were noticably disposed to dispense the charity of the occasion among themselves.

The three clauses which follow (12b-13a) could easily have been written by a resident of western Judea. The clouds which were swept in from the Mediterranean, were so often disappointing, affording no showers for the parched valleys and mountain sides of western Judea. The resulting drouths frequently caused the trees to wither away with their unripe fruit upon them. In such condition they were "doubly dead"— the tree was dead and its fruit was dead, so it presented the dismal aspect of a double death. Along the unprotected coast of western Judea, with no harbors and bays to check the storms of the high seas, the angry waves rolled their frothing crests far up on the beach. If Jude the brother of Jesus wrote this, we may well suppose that he had observed these phenomena in his missionary tours through Judea; if some Jude now unknown to us, we may reasonably consider him to have been a Judean Christian.

The "vagabond stars" were the comets and meteors, which, according to the cosmic conceptions of Jude's day, deserted their proper places in the firmament, soared out in aimless wandering, and finally vanished into eternal darkness beyond the vault of the skies. Inspiration did not correct Jude's cosmology, but secured his accurate representation of redemptive truth. The Holy Spirit was not teaching astronomy through Jude, but redemption.

Another difficulty for the evangelical student lies in verses 14 and 15. We have here a quotation from the apocryphal book known as I Enoch (1:9; 27:2; 60:8). Does this place the endorsement of the Holy Spirit upon I Enoch, or upon these particular passages? Or, if not, does it abnegate the inspiration and canonicity of Jude? Neither conclusion is necessary. We have here again a mere matter of illustrative material, derived from a source familiar to writer and readers, employed for the purpose of enforcing a great truth. The truth illustrated is peril of trifling with the justice and power of God, a truth confirmed by abundant testimony from many other portions of scripture, and sanctioned by the religious mind of all ages. Inspiration guarantees the truth taught, and not the human modes of expression employed in teaching the truth.

A great practical difficulty resulting from the Gnostic agitation is reflected in verse 16. These heretical teachers and their followers were intolerant of the authority of the church officers and the reproach of church discipline. They repudiated such interference with their views and conduct, and proceeded in accordance with their own ideas and preferences. At the same time, they fawned upon the few wealthy members of these early Christian congregations, "flattering vain exhibitions of pride for the sake of personal profit." The wealthy were more susceptible to their arrogant superiority of disposition, and were able to confer generous favors upon them.

In this passage (12-18) Jude presents a very vivid picture of a group of speculative philosophers, proud in their assumption of superior wisdom, but grossly corrupt in their moral conduct. Dualistic Gnostic philosophy is obviously in the background.

Exhortation of the Faithful
Verses 17-23

Jude now turns his attention specifically to those who remained loyal to the truth. We discover here that underneath the rugged nature which, in the preceding verses, was swept by tides of righteous rage, there resided a genuine Christian spirit, which could be placid and gentle and forgiving where such treatment was deserved.

(1) *The Apostolic Warning*, 17-19. Here Jude reminds his readers of the prophetic words of the apostles of Christ, who were accustomed to predict: "At the time of final consummation there shall come mockers, proceeding according to their own evil desires." Almost these exact words occur in II Pt. 3:3, but elsewhere in extant apostolic writings they do not

appear just as Jude gives them here. So Jude and Peter must have given a condensed summary of such predictions as occur in Ac. 20:29, 30; I Tim. 4:1-5; II Tim. 3:1-9; and prophetic elements carried in traditions which long ago have ceased to be used. Doubtless there was a vast amount of traditional material derived from apostolic teaching which was not recorded in the book of Acts. Later reproductions of it are found in at least three extant documents, the "Doctrina," which probably belongs to the end of the first century, and the "Didache" and Barnabas, belonging to the middle of the second century. The full titles of the Doctrina and the Didache really mean "the teaching of the apostles." Other such documents of earlier origin likely perished, and an abundance of such tradition remained unrecorded. Peter and Jude are giving us a brief fragment from this tradition, or possibly from such a document.

Jude considers the false teachers then in the churches to be a fulfillment of this prophecy. "These are the fellows who devise insidious discriminations, being themselves 'psychic' and 'deprived of spiritual nature' " (v. 19). The description of them as psychic, and deprived of spiritual nature, is an echo from their own teaching hurled back at them. Early Gnostics divided human society into three classes, the spiritual, the psychic and the carnal. The spiritual were those entirely emancipated from the bonds of evil matter, and hence saved irrespective of their moral conduct; the psychic were still hampered by the evil flesh, and

JEWISH CHRISTIANITY

saved only if by rigid self-denial they lived pure lives; the carnal were hopelessly enslaved to the flesh, and therefore irrevocably doomed. Jude charges that the Gnostics are really the ones who are "psychic" and "unspiritual."

(2) *The Correct Attitude Toward Error*, 20-23. Jude finally exhorts his readers to establish themselves firmly on a foundation of faith and Spirit-guided prayer, and then manifest a spirit of love and mercy toward the erring. All are not to be dealt with, however, on the same policy. "While on the one hand, you have mercy on those who have grown honestly skeptical, saving them as though snatched from the fire; on the other hand, there will be others toward whom you will exercise mercy with extreme caution, bewaring of the foul contamination of a sensual error" (vs. 22, 23). This is a very free paraphrase from the Greek, but it carries the idea as we discern it in the light of the historical setting. Some who fell into honest doubt, misled and bewildered by the Gnostic confusions, were to be treated with brotherly compassion. But they were in a situation where compassion must be exercised with caution. Some would defiantly persist in the error, and so diabolical and corrupting was this treacherous heresy that the churches could not afford to trifle with it. Obstinate cases must be handled with severe discipline.

Conclusion

Verses 24, 25

Jude closes with a beautiful benediction, which we would render thus: "Now to him who is able to keep you from falling, and to establish you blameless in the presence of his glory in gladness; to the only God our Savior be glory, majesty, might and authority, through Jesus Christ our Lord, through all past eternity, and now, and forevermore. Amen." This benediction is linked up directly with the occasion of the epistle. It offers praise to God as one who is able to keep them pure and true, and insure their ultimate spiritual triumph. Such keeping power was an exceeding comfort to those who were surrounded by a confusing whirl of conflicting teachings and menaced by the subtle temptations which lurked in their pagan environment. The last chord in this diapason of warning carries a note of caution.

CHAPTER VII

THE WIDENING BREACH BETWEEN CHRISTIANITY AND JUDAISM
EPISTLE TO THE HEBREWS

Gentile Christianity has but little recognized the heart pangs which the Christian Jew of the Apostolic Age must have suffered as he beheld himself ever more and more alienated from the religion of his fathers. The one whom he had accepted as his Messiah had been repudiated and executed at the head of Jewish influence—the Sanhedrin at Jerusalem. Rabbinic Judaism had been consistent throughout in its denunciation of the Christian movement. The synagogue as an institution had renounced it, and refused it admission. When we consider the fact that the rabbi and the synagogue were the two most potent factors in Jewish religious life, it is indeed strange that Christianity secured as large Jewish following as it did. Judaism as such rejected the Messiahship of Jesus. By the last quarter of the first century Christianity had become a Gentile religion.

At the same time a revival of traditional Judaism had swept through the Mediterranean world kindling new interest in the ancient views and hopes of Israel. In 70 A. D. the Temple had been destroyed. Consequently there ceased the ritual of the altar and priestly service of ancient Israel, leaving to the synagogue and the rabbi the field of Jewish religion without competition. This awakened a new zeal for the synagogue service, and attached an increased interest to rabbinic instruction and tradition. The Jewish Christian saw this revival sweep through the Jewish world about him, while he could have no share in its enthusiasm. The leaders of Jewish Christianity might have felt no great distress at this loss, but to the average Christian Jew it was undoubtedly a severe trial.

To appreciate the situation thus created we need to take into consideration three facts relative to the first century Jew.

(1) *His Intense Religious Sensibilities.* The Jew felt the hold of his religion upon him as no other race of people ever have. His religion was not only theoretically but actually the biggest thing in his life. It differentiated his nation, it defined his history, it directed his activity. That the religion of Jehovah revealed in the Old Testament was eternally true he never allowed himslf to doubt. Indeed Christianity itself was built upon this premise, for its founder announced himself to be the fulfillment of the hope of deliverance presented in the prophetic message of the Old Testament. Judaism represented to the Jew the perpetuation and defense of the religion of Jehovah. To break away from Judaism was to abandon traditions and practices as sacred as life itself. Therefore to follow a religion which was becoming every day more distinct from Judaism, and threatened more every day the repudiation of Judaism, was of necessity a heartbreaking ordeal to the Jewish Christian.

(2) *His Racial Prejudice.* It was difficult for the Jew to realize that the Gentile stood on an equality with him in the favor of God. He had been trained from infancy to regard the Gentile as a creature on a lower plane of life, morally, religiously and spiritually, than himself. The feeling of the typical Southern white man toward the negro furnishes a very servicable parallel. When the Christian Jew saw his adopted religion drifting constantly farther from the religion of his fathers, and becoming rapidly a distinctly Gentile religion, it placed a terrific strain upon his racial sensibilities.

(3) *His National Hopes.* In home and synagogue it was impressed upon the Jew that his people composed the holy nation of Jehovah's peculiar choice. This fact could but portend a glorious future for the Jewish race as such. The Messiah would come to secure for Israel that supremacy and prosperity which was rightfully his, and which the Gentile conqueror had unjustly—yea, wickedly—snatched from him. Such a thing as a Messiah who would bring favor to the Gentile rather than the Jew was not only absurd; it was positively sacrilegious. The glory of Israel was the promise of Jehovah, and therefore must be the chief aim of the Messiah whom He would send. This eventual triumph of God's elect was the dearest hope in the heart of the devout Jew. For the Messiah to be gradually drawn away from the Jew, to become the peculiar benefactor of the Gentile, was a development very difficult for the Jew to comprehend.

By 75 A. D. the religion of Jesus had become distinctively and predominantly Gentile. In nearly all the churches outside Palestine the Gentile constituency was far in the majority. Gentile conceptions and terminology were used as means of expression for Christian teaching. The leaders and teachers in the churches were largely Gentile, the Jewish nucleus having dwindled almost to the vanishing point.

The interest of the Christian movement had become preponderantly Gentile. The chief concern of the churches and their leaders was the evangelization of the Gentile world, rather than the elevation of the Jew to his rightful place as God's elect. To this aim and endeavor the Christian Jew was expected to contribute heartily and sacrificially. It is hardly conceivable that this should not have laid a severe strain upon his Jewish conscience and painfully wounded his Jewish sensibilities.

The situation in the last quarter of the first century was obviously exasperating to the Christian Jew. Bewilderment, misgiving and regret were the inevitable result. It is probable that during this crisis dissolution threatened many Jewish churches. That at least one congregation in Rome passed through such a crucial reaction is reflected in the Epistle to the Hebrews. To understand this Epistle, that situation of the widening breach between Christianity and Judaism must be recognized and constantly kept in mind. It is against this background that we undertake here the interpretation of the epistle.

HEBREWS

This epistle is a striking literary product. Attention is arrested at the very beginning by the absence of any salutation, an element so characteristic of New Testament epistles. Only this epistle and I John lack salutations. It has been truly said of Hebrews that it begins like a treatise, proceeds like a sermon, and closes like an epistle. It is more in the nature of a doctrinal treatise than any other book in the New Testament, being approached in this respect only by Romans. The author was an exceedingly versatile individual. He shows a marvelously comprehensive grasp of the Old Testament and the essential content of Judaism, and yet is quite clearly at home in the field of Hellenistic Jewish literature and Alexandrian thought. He exhibits a masterly command of the Greek language and a splendid rhetorical style. He is at the same time a mighty logician, and has produced one of the most convincing arguments ever put into literary form. His book is an invincible proof of the superiority of Chirst to the Old Testament regime.

(1) *Composition.* As to who the author was we do not know, and there is no way of finding out with any degree of certainty. Ancient tradition ascribes it to both Paul and Barnabas. The latter has the stronger claim, for the tradition favoring him first appears with more confidence than that favoring Paul, and the epistle is too widely different from anything Paul wrote to be thought of as coming from him. Yet that Barnabas wrote it is quite improbable. Of the

many guesses at the author that have been hazarded doubtless the most plausible is Apollos. The suggestion is based upon a comparison of the characteristics of the epistle with the description of Apollos in Ac. 18:24, where he is spoken of as a fluent man, and "mighty in the scriptures." The book of Hebrews presents an extraordinary command of language, and employs the Old Testament scriptures more freely than any other book of the New Testament, just the features which harmonize with Luke's description of Apollos. But this cannot be received as more than a plausible suggestion.

The place of composition is in even greater obscurity. It is not worth our while even to hazard a guess on that question.

As to date, the epistle gives fairly convincing clues. It appears to have been written after the destruction of Jerusalem for it contemplates the Tabernacle ritual of the Pentateuch rather than the Temple ritual of Judaism. We shall find that the evident occasion of the book fits well into the rabbinic revival which followed the destruction of the Temple, and this could not have begun earlier than 75 or 80. The epistle is quoted freely in I Clement, which was written at Rome about 97 A. D. These considerations would place the writing of Hebrews within the last quarter of the first century.

There appears another important feature of internal evidence which helps us toward fixing the date still more definitely. It appears that the readers had already passed through a period of persecution a considerable time before (10:32-34), which we may most reasonably consider to have been the Neronian persecution. When the book was written they were being threatened with another persecution (12:4-13), which was most probably that under Domitian. Now we know that in the early years of Domitian's reign his attention was not attracted to the Christians. The earliest signs of disfavor appear along toward 90 A.D. Consequently we would place the date of Hebrews at 85 to 90 A. D.

(2) *Occasion.* The epistle was addressed to a group of Jewish Christians, probably in Rome. The correct rendering of the final sentence in 13:24 is, "Those from Italy salute you." This is not conclusive evidence by any means, but suggests that associates of the writer from Rome were sending greetings back to those at home. However, the location of the writers is immaterial in the interpretation of the epistle. The matter of real interest is their situation and experience.

They had been in the past conspicuous for their fidelity and generosity (6:10, 11; 10:32-35). But their former enthusiasm had waned, and they were growing impatient under the strain of threatened persecution. It is possible that they were somewhat disappointed in their eschatological expectations. The Messiah had not returned to earth "to restore the kingdom to Israel," and called home the Diaspora, as they had anticipated. Jesus hardly seemed to have proved out to be the Messiah of Israel, but had been changed into a redeemer-god of the Gentiles, and Christianity appeared to Jewish eyes as more a Gentile religious cult than the kingdom of Jehovah. Their own countrymen doubtless ridiculed them because of their religious disappointments, and the line of cleavage between Chirstianity and Judaism was clearly growing more marked every day. They felt that the time had come when they must decide between the religion of their fathers, held in holy bonds for centuries of sacred history, and a new Messianism which inevitably appeared to them as being rapidly transformed into a Gentile cult. At least they must find some means of bringing their particular form of Christianity nearer to Judaism.

The rabbinic revival which ensued upon the destruction of the Temple was calculated to increase their dissatisfaction. While the tides were ebbing ever lower in Jewish Christianity, they were sweeping out with increasing power in synagogue Judaism. The church services had lost their fervor and enthusiasm, and the synagogue services had taken on new zeal. This would obviously lay a strain on the faith and fidelity of the Jewish Christians.

Historical evidence is strong that an abortive form of Christianity arose among the Palestinian churches, slowly spreading into the Hellenistic world and issuing in the Ebionites of the second century. There is no question that Palestinian Christianity exercised an increasing influence over the Jewish churches of the Dispersion, and the Palestinian churches drew ever farther away from Gentile Christianity. It is quite probable that this influence had reached the readers of Hebrews.

The author of Hebrews has been intimately associated with this group of Jewish Christians (13:19). He is still loyal to God's revelation of Himself in the Old Testament, and sees in Christianity, not the displacement of Judaism, but its ultimate fulfillment. He is utterly devoted to Christ and his universal program of redemption, and is here pouring out his heart in a mighty and eloquent appeal to his kinsmen to persist in their fidelity to the Christian religion undiminished and unmodified. David Smith fittingly describes the epistle as "a message of reassurance, demonstrating from their sacred Scriptures that in embracing the Gospel they had lost nothing but rather gained immeasurably, since they had exchanged symbol for reality, shadow for substance; and, moreover, that in suffering for Christ they were treading the path which the saints of old, Israel's heroes of faith, had trodden from generation to generation." (*Disciple's Commentary,* vol. v, p. 319.)

We have here the last heroic effort in that pathetic struggle of the apostolic group to retain Judaism in the bonds of Christ. The same tragic situation which called forth Paul's heart-broken cry in Rom. 9:1ff. is likewise reflected in the tears which gleam in every verse of Hebrews. Israel had renounced the glory of his own heritage, and was stubbornly groping away ever deeper into the gloom, while a few loving hearts mourned in anguish his direful fate. It was to such baffled, bleeding hearts that the writer of Hebrews poured forth his innermost soul, in a courageous effort to call them back to the fervor of their former zeal.

(3) *Structure.* There is to be found rather general agreement among commentators that Hebrews presents two main divisions. There is first a great argument wherein the writer seeks to prove the superiority of Christ to the old order. This argumentative portion embraces chapters 1:1 to 10:18. From 10:19 to the end of the book we have the practical application of its great conclusion that Christ is superior and sufficient. Hence argument and application constitute the chief divisions of the epistle. On this basis we offer the following outline.

I. *Argument,* 1:1-10:18.

   Christ superior to the old order in:

   1. Revelation, 1:1-2:18.
      (1) Superior to the prophetic revelation, 1:1-3.
      (2) Superior to the angelic revelation, 1:4-2:18.
         i. In his essential character, 1:5-14.
            (Parenthetical exhortation, 2:1-4.)
         ii. In his redemptive function, 2:5-18.

   2. Administration, 3:1-4:13.
      (1) Superior in his relation to the task, 3:1-4.
      (2) Superior in the capacity in which he serves, 3:5-14.
      (3) Superior in the results accomplished, 3:15-4:13.

3. Mediation, 4:14-10:18.
 (1) Superior in qualifications, 4:14-7:25.
   i. As to his human contact, 4:14-5:3.
     ii. As to his divine appointment, 5:4-7:25.
       i. His priesthood obediently accepted, 5:4-10. (Parenthetical, 5:11-6:20).
       ii. His priesthood supplants the Aaronic, 7:1-10.
     iii. His priesthood final and eternal, 7:11-25.
 (2) Superior in character, 7:26-8:5.
   i. He was sinless, 7:26-28.
   ii. He was divine, 8:1-5.
 (3) Superior in ministry, 8:6-10:18.
   i. Based upon a better covenant, 8:6-13.
   ii. Performed through a better service, 9:1-22.
   iii. Accomplished by a better sacrifice, 9:23-10:18.
     i. Offered in the presence of God, 9:24.
     ii. Offered once for all, 9:25-10:18.

II. *Application,* 10:19-13:17.
 1. Courage, 10:19-38.
 (1) A word of exhortation, 10:19-25.
 (2) A word of warning, 10:26-31.
 (3) A word of reminder, 10:32-38.
 2. Faith, 10:39-11:40.
 (1) The achievements of faith, 10:39-11:12.
 (2) The submissiveness of faith, 11:13-40.
 3. Fortitude, 12:1-13.
 (1) Because of a heritage of sacrificial faith, 12:1.

(2) Because of the example of Jesus, 12:2,3.
(3) Because of their relation to God, 12:4-13.
4. Holiness, 12:14-13:17.
(1) The meaning of holiness, 12:14-17.
(2) The incentives of holiness, 12:18-29.
(3) The practice of holiness, 13:1-17.
   i. An altruistic spirit, 13:1-3.
   ii. Domestic integrity, 13:4.
   iii. Freedom from avarice, 13:5-7.
   iv. Faithfulness in religious duties, 13:8-17.

Conclusion 13:18-25

The course of the writer's thought as thus analyzed we seek to follow through his remarkable logical discussion. We will of course find points at which the progress of the thought is difficult to discern, and much is left to the arbitrary choice of the interpreter. There is as little of this obscurity of logical sequence, however, in Hebrews as anywhere in the New Testament. It compares favorably with Romans in symmetry of structure.

ARGUMENT

1:1-10:18

One's impression of the cogency of this argument will depend on whether he considers it in the light of its own times, or measures it by the present day standards of argumentation and debate. Those critics who cast aspersions on the strength of the argument in Hebrews are submitting it to the exacting tests of their own scientific age. This is not correct historical interpretation. If we weigh the arguments of the book from the viewpoint of their own efficiency in the thought of the first century Jewish readers, there cannot be found a more convincing argument in human literature. It is therefore imperative that we keep in mind that the argument is addressed to first century Christian Jews.

It is profoundly interesting to note that the author in his argument builds upon the three essential elements of Jewish religion. (i) The Old Testament scriptures, the "Law", lay at the foundation of Judaism. (ii) The administration of this Law in the application of the Mosaic code was the next matter of concern to the Jew. The name Moses represented supreme authority in earthly affairs for Judaism. (iii) Then there was the worship of Jehovah, carried on first in the Tabernacle, and afterward across many centuries of Hebrew history in the Temple. In this worship the priesthood and sacrifice, as means of propitiation, were the essential elements. That is, the three fundamentals in the religion of Judaism were revelation, administration, mediation. Around these three fundamentals our author builds his argument.

Revelation, 1:1-2:18

In Jewish thinking there had been two mediums of revelation. Preeminent in Jewish Christian thought was the word of the prophet, doubtless for two reasons. The prophets presented the most spiritual message of the Old Testament, and apostolic Christianity inherited from its Lord an intense interest in the spiritual.

Furthermore, it was the prophets who offered a word of scriptural authority for the ministry and religion of Christ. But the Christian Jew also respected the other portions of the Old Testament, which were popularly believed to have been mediated through angels. The writer shows that Jesus was superior to both these modes of revelation.

(1) *Superior to the Prophetic Revelation*, 1:1-3. These verses contain the main thesis, and might be regarded as a general prologue to the whole epistle. It is, as A. B. Bruce observes, "the portico of an august temple, its weighty clauses being a row of stately ornamental pillars supporting the roof" (*The Epistle to the Hebrews,* p. 26). "God having long ago, in many portions and in many ways, spoken unto the fathers by the prophets, in the days of the consummation spoke unto us in the person of a Son, whom he constituted as heir of all things and through whom he laid out the plan of the ages; who being the effulgence of his glory and the exact expressiion of his essential being, also sustaining all things by the word of his power, having made purification of sins, sat down on the right hand of the Majesty on high." The central idea is, "God hath spoken". The author of Hebrews thinks of revelation as God speaking to men. Notice his characteristic way of introducing his scripture quotations with some form of the verb "say". He is giving in these verses a comparison of two types or methods of revelation. It is the first of many such contrasts found in this epistle, the key word of which is "better". Christ is better

than the prophetic revelation. The older revelation was in fragmentary messages, delivered in various ways through the prophets. God's final method is to reveal Himself, not through a prophet, but through a Son. Christ was God's final and supreme revelation. Then the contrast set forth in this passage is the diversity and incompleteness of the prophetic method of revelation as compared with that which we have in Christ.

i. The prophets at best were no more than servants of Jehovah, while Christ was a Son, the appointed heir of all things, the agent of God's redemptive plan.

ii. The message of the prophets had looked on into the future for the ultimate realization of God's plan, while in Christ God spoke "at the end of these days". Here we have that Greek phrase *ep'eschatou* which refers to the consummation of the age, which to the Jew was the era ushered in by the advent of the Messiah. David Smith recognizes that "the phrase signifies in Jewish parlance the times of the Messiah" (*Disciple's Commentary*, in loco). The prophets spoke long before the realization of God's purpose of deliverance; Christ spoke from the midst of its fulfillment.

iii. The prophets were but mere mortals, while Christ was (to paraphrase from the Greek) the light shed forth by the glory of God and the exact expression of His essential being; the one perpetuating the physical universe by the word of God's power and saving the spiritual universe by the consummation of his redemptive career; that is, by having accomplished purification for sin on the cross, and having ascended to glory at the right hand of God.

Thus in at least three points of pronounced contrast Christ as a medium of revelation was superior to the prophets.

(2) *Superior to the Angelic Revelation*, 1:4-2:18. The ministry of angels held a very high place in the religious contemplation of first century Judaism. A basis for the conception is found in the Old Testament, but the Jews had exaggerated and embellished the ministry of angels far beyond the simple Old Testament conception. They were now thought of as the chief means of mediation between God and men, and therefore indispensable in revelation. It was angels who gave the revelation to Moses, and Moses passed it on to Israel. The author of Hebrews does not either condemn or sanction this view, but simply proves that Christ supersedes the angelic function, in whatever light it may be conceived. If he is thus so far superior to the angels, then his religion must be superior to the provisional religion which the angels revealed to Moses.

i. Jesus is superior to the angels in the essential character which has been ascribed to him (1:5-2:4). When the author says, "having become superior to the angels in the measure that the name which he has inherited presents a superior excellence as compared with them," he is using a distinctively Jewish form of expression. To the Jew a name was much more than a mere designation of identity; it was a description of character. So a greatly superior name meant greatly superior character. Three scriptural proofs are presented to show that Christ has inherited a more excellent name than the angels.

(i) According to the plain statement of scripture, Christ had been exalted to the dignity of a Son, which honor no angel ever received (v. 5). The word Son in the Greek receives special emphasis, being found at the beginning of the quotation, which reads literally (we reproduce the emphasis with italics), "*Son* of mine art thou". Instead of receiving any such exalted name, angels have been commanded to worship the Son (v. 6). This verse looks forward to the Second Advent. The word rendered "world" means the inhabited world, human society. The Son became a member of human society once, in the Incarnation; he shall return to enter human society again in the Parousia. The clause may be rendered, "Now when again he ushers in the First-born into human society, etc". The thought is familiar to the readers, that in the final triumph of Messiah all the moral creation, men and angels, are to offer him their homage. This would indicate most forcefully to the Jewish mind the superiority of the Son.

(ii) The essential superiority of the Son to the angels is revealed in the relative position assigned to them in the universe (1:7-12). According to the scripture, the angels have been assigned to a place of servitude, for God is described as "making His angels winds, and His ministrants a flame of fire" (v. 7). In the Jewish view, since God as pure Spirit could not have contact with the material universe, He used the angelic creation to administer cosmic affairs. Far from being on a par with the Son as objects of worship, they were assigned to menial tasks in the performance of mundane functions. God employed them as the spiritual agencies behind the forces of nature (cf. Dods, *The Expositor's Greek Testament*, in loco). The quotation used here is the Septuagint rendering of Ps. 104:4, which reads according to the literal rendering of the Hebrew, "who maketh winds his messengers, and flaming fire his ministers". One will find theological difficulty here only if he wishes to regard the Bible as a manual of natural science and a standard of literary criticism, neither of which it was divinely designed to be. This verse is not to be taken as endorsing the accuracy of either Septuagint translation or Jewish cosmic conceptions. It is meant to reveal the eternal and unrivalled superiority of our Lord.

In contrast with the menial servitude of the angels, the Son has been recognized by scripture as a divine sovereign (vs. 8, 9). It is interesting to note how the author here takes a scripture in which the object of adoration is called God and ascribes it to the Messiah. It is one of the many evidences in the book of Hebrews that the author believed in the deity of Christ. In verses 10 to 12 divine functions and attributes are ascribed to the Son. He is the author of the created universe (v. 10), and is eternal and immutable in character (vs. 11, 12). Only real Deity could fill such a role.

(*iii*) The scriptures describe the ultimate exaltation of the Son in such way as to establish beyond doubt his superiority to the angelic creation (1:13, 14). Christ has been exalted to the place of supreme honor at the right hand of God, there to await ultimate triumph (v. 13); while angels have been subordinated even to the followers of Christ (v. 14). This place of inferiority even to believers is possible to all the angelic creation, and not to some of the lowest orders. "Are they not *all* ministering spirits, commissioned for service on behalf of those who are destined to inherit salvation " This verse clearly teaches that the angelic creation as a whole is inferior to the redeemed of the human race. This is in accord with God's creative purposes, for Psalms 8:5, correctly rendered, says of man, "For thou hast made him a little lower than God." In the original purpose of God, man was to be next to His own divine status of being. Sin destroyed man's transcendent character, but redemption restores him to his rightful place, and angels again became his servile subordinates.

(*Parenthetical*, 2:1-4.) In these verses the superiority of Christ to the angels is used as the predicate for a very forceful word of warning. If a revelation mediated through angels received the sanction of divine retribution upon any who disregarded it, how much more shall a revelation through the Son, who is so highly exalted above the angels, receive the sanction of an unrelenting justice. Then the readers should beware that they do not disregard this salvation.

The passage is introduced with one of the strongest inferential particles in the Greek language. It throws this warning back with intense emphasis upon the preceding argument that Christ in his essential character is better than the angels. The writer has shown in the first chapter how the scriptures indicate the Messiah to be a reigning judge, an honored favorite in courts divine, creator of the universe, the unchanging God, the exalted, triumphant Son. In view of this the readers should take firm hold upon the things in which they have been instructed by their Christian teachers, lest by any means they should let slip the moorings of faith and drift with the tides of indifference and unbelief.

The word in verse 1 translated "give heed" in our English version means literally to hold firmly, to cling to tenaciously. The word rendered "drift away" means to float or glide by, as of a boat which has broken from its moorings and drifted helplessly upon the high seas. The moorings of these Christian Jews were the "things heard"; the traditions which had been taught them by their early Christian teachers. The apparent danger is that the readers will repudiate these teachings and drift with the tides of doubt and uncertainty.

The writer seeks to convince his readers that it is a perilous course they are threatening to take (vs.

2, 3a). We may paraphrase the Greek as follows: "For if the message spoken through angelic mediation became so solemnly confirmed, and every sin, whether of malicious intent or of human weakness, received its merited retribution, how shall we (who have received such a superior revelation as that in Christ) escape if we lose interest in such a great salvation?" The great danger seems to have been, not that they would repudiate the salvation of Christ and abandon it, but that confusion and disappointment would destroy their loyalty and devotion to it. The word rendered "neglect" means to lose care for, to become indifferent toward.

To allow such a condition to develop would be exceedingly unwise, in view of the abundant endorsement which the Christian revelation had received. The redemptive message had received its original declaration by the Lord himself; literally, "having received a beginning by being spoken through the Lord" (v. 3). It was then transferred to the author and his readers by the apostolic teachers, being to them the sure word of the Master because received from those who heard him teach.

Thus the message they had received had its apostolic endorsement. But it also had its divine endorsement (v. 4). God bestowed His divine sanction upon the Christian revelation in the form of signs and wonders and varied miracles, and by distribution of the Spirit's power, according to His will.

ii. Jesus is superior to the angels in the *redemptive function* which has been assigned to him (2:5-18).

The writer has been considering the relative position of Christ and the angels in the past; he now turns to the future to speak of their relative place in "the world to come" (v. 5). The term here rendered "world" refers to organized human society. There is eventually to come a new world order of redeemed society, and angels have been assigned no place of superiority in it. This point he now proposes to prove: "concerning which we are going to speak" (construing the verb for "speak" as a futuristic present in the Greek).

The writer finds a passage in the Psalms (8:4ff.) presenting the exaltation of man in the divine purpose of creation which declares, "And didst set him over the works of thy hands; Thou didst put all things in subjection under his feet" (vs. 7c, 8a). The writer sees the significant point here in the expression "all things". He infers from this that there is nothing which is not to be subject to man, according to the divine purpose (v. 8b). But man, as we see him on earth, is far from possessing such a prerogative. "But up to the present, we do not yet see 'all things subjected' to him" (v. 8c). Does this mean that God's purpose in creation has been thwarted? No; it only means that Christ had to accomplish on man's behalf the fulfillment of this original design of creation (v. 9).

But in order to achieve this divine purpose for man, Christ must needs participate in the lot and nature of man.

(*i*) He must partake of the lot of man through

suffering. "For it became Him, who was the original reason and agent of all creation, in bringing a redeemed race up to the plane of His divine purpose, to perfect the author of their salvation through sufferings" (v. 10). The sufferings of Christ extended in two directions: they enabled man to reach up to God, and they enabled God to reach down to man.

(*ii*) He must partake of the lot of man through humiliation (vs. 11-13). "Moreover, the one who redeems and those being redeemed are all of one nature" (v. 11). The word rendered "sanctify" in our English version embraces that entire process of grace by which the believing soul is separated from sin and devoted to the purposes of redemption. We therefore render it by the broader term redeem. That the Messiah voluntarily humbled himself and shared man's nature as a brother human, the writer proves by three citations from the Old Testament (vs. 11*b*-13).

(*iii*) He must partake of man's lot by sharing the dread experience of death (vs. 14, 15). "Furthermore, since those who are children partake of blood and flesh, he himself also shared with them in an intimate fellowship, in order that through death he might vanquish him who has the power of death; that is, the devil" (v. 14). He shared thus in man's struggle with his last great enemy, that he might become the victor over death and liberate man from its bondage.

Such a mission the Messiah has in no sense wrought for angels, but for "the seed of Abraham" (v. 16), to which class the readers belonged. Again the subordination of the angelic creation to the heirs of grace is indicated. Christ submitted himself to man's humiliation and suffering, condescending to become the brother of man, in order that, as a faithful high-priest, he might lead man back to God, and to the high and holy destiny for which God intended him. He descended to a human status in order that he might rescue human life and restore it to its high estate in the ultimate purpose of God.

Administration, 3:1-4:13

In 3:1,2 the author introduces the two chief elements around which the remainder of his argument is to revolve: the ideas of apostleship and priesthood. The word apostle means one sent (Gk., *apostlos*), and signifies one commissioned to the performance of a definite task, one authorized by another. The development of the subsequent context makes it certain that Moses is here in mind. His commission as an "apostle", representative of divine authority, may be found in Exodus 3:10, where in the Septuagint text the verb form of the word apostle occurs. God sent Moses as an apostle ("apostolized" him, if we may coin a word to better represent the Greek) to deliver the children of Israel out of bondage in Egypt, and form into a nation for Him. He sent ("apostolized") Jesus to deliver the elect out of the bondage of sin and form them into a redeemed race. Both had consigned to them a task of administration. The author proceeds to compare the success of Moses with that of Christ. He shows that the superiority of Christ consisted in:

(1) *His Relation to the Task,* 3:3, 4. The writer says of Christ (paraphrasinig from the Greek), "For he is to be judged as worthy of an honor superior to that of Moses by just that degree in which the one who builds a house is worthy of more honor than the house he builds." Moses was but one of the nation which he sought to establish for God, and hence part of the house that he was helping to build. Christ was the original power and authority in establishing a redeemed nation for God. He is as much greater than Moses as the architect is greater than the structure which he erects. Since the readers acknowledged Christ to be the true Messiah of Israel, they could not deny this contention. The author clinches his argument by the observation that a house must have somebody to build it, it cannot build itself; while God is the original builder, the implication is that Jesus, being divine, shares in this original relation to the task.

(2) *The Capacity in Which He Serves,* 3:5,6. Verses 5 and 6 may be rendered thus: "And while Moses was faithful *in* all God's house as one *serving* for a witness of those things which were to be revealed, yet Christ occupies a place *over* God's house as a *Son.* We constitute this house of God, as long as we cling unfailingly to our confidence and the boast of our hope clear out to the very end." Moses labored as a *servant,* but Christ as a *Son.* Moses served *in* God's house, while Christ reigns *over* it. Hence to reject the authority of Christ is far more serious than to reject the authority of Moses.

222   JEWISH CHRISTIANITY

(3) *The Results Accomplished*, 3:7-4:13. Here is the writer's most convincing argument for the superiority of Christ over the Mosaic administration, so in logical consistency he devotes far more space to it. Be it observed, there are contentions advanced here which must have shocked inherent Jewish sensibilities.

The writer begins this part of his argument by laying a scriptural predicate, as is his custom. His confidence in the divine authority of his premise is disclosed in the first clause (v. 7a), "Wherefore, as the Holy Spirit says". The word rendered "wherefore" is a strong inferential particle. The writer believes that only the inadequacy of Moses to the final achievements of redemption could reasonably account for what is here said by the Psalmist.

Before proceeding to expound his scriptural predicate in its application to the point at issue, the writer, as so often in this book, drops in a parenthetical word of exhortation (3:12-14). The message of prophesy implies a solemn warning to his readers, declaring that "today" (which the author construes as refering to the Messianic age) God will not be so longsuffering toward backsliding as He had been in the past. If God punished those who were disloyal to the leadership of Moses, how much more shall He punish those who desert the leadership of His Son Jesus Christ?

There are two significant points found by the author in his scriptural predicate, implied in two of its statements. The first is, "Today, if you will hear his voice, harden not your hearts, as in the provocation, on the day of trial in the wilderness, where your fathers tried me in a demonstration, and saw the manifestations of my providence for forty years: wherefore, I was displeased with that generation" (vs. 7-10a); the second, "They shall not enter into my rest" (v. 11b). These statements of scripture suggest to the mind of the author that Moses failed to accomplish the perfect realization of redemption at two points.

i. He failed to *preserve a perfect following* (3:15 -4:2). The writer calls attention to the evident fact that the Psalm quoted, which plainly indicated that certain ones had fallen short of the promised goal, had reference to the children of Israel as led by Moses. "When it says, 'Today, if you will hear his voice, harden not your hearts, as in the day when you provoked him', who was it that having heard 'provoked him'? It was, was it not, all those who came out of Egypt under the leadership of Moses? And with whom was God 'displeased for forty years'? Why of course it was those who sinned, was it not, whose bodies fell in the wilderness? And to whom did he 'swear that they should not enter into his rest', if not to those who were disbelieving?" (vs. 15-18).

The Greek presents in the form of rhetorical questions a very emphatic affirmation that it was those led by Moses who fell short. "So we observe that they were unable to 'enter in' on account of their unbelieving disobedience" (v. 19). Their unbelieving disobedience (the Greek word carries both ideas) caused them to fail to find in the Promised Land the promised Rest. Hence Moses did not accomplish a perfect deliverance. This inference would startle a Jewish reader, but the author presents it in a way that makes it indisputable. To a Jewish Christian reader it must have been profoundly impressive. Why hold on to Moses in preference to Christ, when Moses had failed of a perfect realization of the goal of redemption?

Feeling the significance of this thought for his readers, the writer inserts a word of exhortation and application (4:1,2). These hortatory parentheses, which occur so frequently in this book, lead one to believe that the author was a preacher, and here addressing himself to a familiar audience. "Therefore let us fear," he admonished, "lest, a promise having remained over unfulfilled for us 'to enter into rest,' any of you should turn up disqualified for it" (v. 1). The point is, that in view of the fact that Moses failed to realize the perfect fruition of the divine promise of deliverance, and it consequently remains accessible to their own generation as yet unfulfilled, the readers should be greatly concerned that they do not, as Israel of old, fall short of the necessary qualifications. If so, they too will miss the promise. Let them therefore beware that they manifest a spirit of obedient faith. "For indeed, we have had the gospel preached to us even as also they; but the imparted message did not profit them, because, in those who heard, it was not mixed with faith" (v. 2). The gospel of redemption has been continuous, from the time of Israel's unfortunate experience to the present heirs of promise; and the condition of its reception ever remains the same—faith in the hearts of those who hear. This is a pungent warning to wavering Jewish Christians.

ii. The writer deals now with the second inference from his scriptural predicate, "They shall not enter into my rest" (3:11b). Moses failed to *achieve the ultimate aim* of the promise (4:3-13). Being yet unattained, it is still reserved for those who believe. If the readers will remain faithful, and exercise true, persistent faith they will inherit the promised Rest, since it still remains. "For it is we who have believed who are to enter into the Rest, for this reason: He said, 'As I swore in my wrath, they shall not enter into my Rest'" (v. 3). Moses was unable, due to the unbelief of Israel, to lead them to this final Rest. But they cannot therefore indifferently dismiss the matter. This Rest has its revealed place as an essential part of God's redemptive plan of the ages (vs. 3b-5). Commenting on the last clause of verse 3, "As I swore in my wrath, they shall not enter into my Rest; although the works were finished from the foundation of the world," Marcus Dods says, "This quotation confirms the first clause of the verse because it proves two things: first, that God had a rest, and second, that He intended that man should rest with Him, because it was 'in His wrath', justly excited against the unbeliever, . . . that He sware they should not enter in. Had it not been God's original purpose and desire that men should enter into His rest, it could not be said that 'in wrath' He excluded some. Their failure to secure rest was not due to the nonexistence of any rest, for God's works were finished when the world was founded. This is confirmed by Scripture, ... where it is said that after the six days of creation God rested on the seventh day from all His works. That God has a rest is also stated in the ninety-fifth Psalm, for these words 'they shall not enter into my rest' prove that God had a rest" (*Expositor's Greek Testament, in loco.*) Hence it is established by scripture that Moses failed to attain the ultimate aim of redemptive purpose, which was the promised Rest.

It is therefore a resultant fact that the Rest still remains for someone, for whom in the purpose of God it was really intended. "Since therefore it is left for somebody to enter it, and those formerly receiving a gospel did not enter on account of disobedience, again he defineth a certain day by the term 'Today' when he says in David after so long a time (as above cited), 'Today if you will hear his voice, harden not your hearts'" (vs. 6, 7). The fact that away down in the time of David such a Rest is promised is conclusive evidence that when Joshua led the children of Israel into Canaan he did not lead them into the promised Rest. The King James Version says in verse 8, "For if Jesus had given them Rest," but this is a palpable mistranslation of the Greek ('Ιησοῦς), which is a transliteration of the Aramaic form of Joshua, and here clearly refers, not to our Lord, but to the ancient leader of Israel. The verse should read, "For if Joshua had lead them into final Rest, after his period of history the Psalmist would not have spoken of another day." There is a considerable element of paraphrase in this rendering, but we believe it gives the correct sense.

The opportunity therefore remains for Christ to accomplish that in which Moses failed. "Therefore, Sabbath-rest for God's people remains over as not yet fulfilled" (v. 9). But the readers are to be warned by the example of disobedient Israel, for, as the Greek of verses 12 and 13 literally means, God is rigidly discriminating in His reckoning and subtly discerning in His estimate of those with whom He deals.

The rendering "the word of God" has obscured the real meaning of verse 12. This rendering unjustly interrupts the connection with the context. The writer is not here turning aside from the original sequence of his discussion to make an observation relative to the Bible, nor is he adopting a Johannine form of terminology and offering a parenthetical description of Christ. He is following consistently and faithfully the line of his argument. The term here rendered "word" (*logos*) also means a reckoning, a calling into account. It is found in the papyri in commercial documents, where it is used of an account or calculation in business. Hence it may mean a reckoning by thorough examination. That is decidedly the best understanding of the word in this connection. The author is warning his readers not to trifle with God, for His reckoning is vital and active, discriminating in the most exacting way. The word rendered "sword" is used in Greek literature of the surgeon's knife, and such it seems to mean here.

God's discriminating judgment pierces like the surgeon's lancet; even as the surgeon's lancet would if it were separating the very joints and probing even to the marrow within the bone. Hence the readers had better beware how they trifle with His redemptive plans.

We believe that verses 12 and 13 are brought more in line with the context when translated thus: "God's reckoning is vital and active, and sharper than a double edged lancet, even piercing to the point of dividing soul and spirit, joints and marrow, and holding to account the inclinations and purposes of the heart; and no created thing is concealed from his sight, but everything is naked and laid out prostrate before the eyes of Him before whom we have to give account". It would appear then that in these verses we have God's penetrative and discriminative judgment presented under the figure of an exploratory surgical operation: the picture of a patient, stripped and laid out upon the operating table, subjected to the keen lancet and practiced eye of the surgeon. Archaeological and paleographical sources have furnished abundant evidence of the remarkably high development of medical and surgical science in the Graeco-Roman world, and here we have a trace of it in the New Testament.

Mediation, 4:14-10:18

Having disposed of the question of apostleship, the author now turns to the other matter introduced in 3:1, the idea of priesthood. This is by far the longest section of the epistle, and embraces its distinctive theme. The priesthood of Christ marks this epistle as does no other thought. While the present section is devoted exclusively to its consideration, the idea is woven into many other places (e. g., 1:3; 2:10, 17; 12:24; 13:10-12, etc.)

Our writer shows his Jewish readers that Christ is superior to the Aaronic priesthood in three fundamental respects: in qualifications, in character, and in ministry.

(1) *In Qualifications*, 4:14-7:25. It is probably not merely incidental that the writer gives so much space to the question of qualifications for the priesthood, for in Jewish law and practice it held a relatively high place. Judaism insisted that its priests be properly qualified, and there were elaborate qualifications prescribed. But while the qualifications upon which the Jews insisted were largely lineal and ceremonial, our author presents qualifications which are moral and spiritual. He reveals in this fact by a perhaps unconscious implication the essential superiority of Christianity to Judaism. He clearly presents these qualifications, however, with great confidence, for they are prerequisites which are obviously necessary. By the very nature of his office a priest must have a human relationship and a divine relationship, for he approaches God on behalf of man.

i.. In order to function effectively a priest must have an effective *human contact* (4:14-5:3). Though divine, Christ meets also this requirement, for he had in a real and sufficient measure the necessary human touch. "Having therefore a highpriest who has passed through the heavens, Jesus the Son of God, let us remain loyal to our confession: for we have not an highpriest who is incapable of sympathizing with our human weaknesses, but one who has been tempted in every way in a similar manner, *without sin*" (vs. 14, 15). There is no question about his being divine, for he has "passed through the heavens". In the Jewish view of the heavenly realm, the top-most heaven was the dwelling-place of God Himself; so having "passed through the heavens" Jesus penetrated to the most exalted sphere of being, rightfully attaining this exaltation, for he was "Jesus the Son of God". And this also preserves for him another distinction as priest. "As the Aaronic High Priest passed through the veil, or . . . through the various fore courts, into the holiest place, so this great High Priest had passed through the heavens and appeared among eternal realities" (Dods, *op. cit.*). He therefore deserves all the trust that one may repose in divinity and priestly dignity. But this does not remove him from the possibilities of sympathizing with poor weak sinners, for "he has been tempted in every particular in a similar manner". But in this capacity he possesses a transcendent advantage over the Aaronic priesthood. He is entirely capable of sympathizing with all the weaknesses and trials of those for whom he ministers as highpriest, but he is himself without sin. The emphasis on this phrase, indicated by position in the Greek, we have sought to reproduce by emphatic type in English. It is the point of special stress, the point of superiority over the Aaronic priesthood.

Again in verse 16 the author turns aside from the progress of his argument for a brief preachment. Having the mediation of such a highpriest, divine in prerogatives and human in experiences, we can approach the throne of grace with unfaltering confidence.

At 5:1 the writer returns to the course of his argument, and looks at the other side of his present proposition. The Christian's highpriest is without sin, but not so with the Aaronic highpriest. He can qualify abundantly on the human contact, for he is "taken from among men", and is appointed to function at God's altar "on behalf of men"; he is "able to bear with the ignorant and erring", being himself "encompassed with infirmity" (v. 2). Nevertheless, he can only approach God as a sinner, with sin offerings for himself as well as the people (v. 3). Then Jesus is superior to the Aaronic highpriest in that he has just as effective contact with human experience, but is himself without sin.

ii. It is necessary that a priest should receive his office through *divine appointment* (5:4-7:25), and not assume it as a matter of personal choice. "Furthermore, one does not voluntarily appropriate this office, but is called by God, as indeed was Aaron" (v. 4). It was believed by the Jews that Aaron had a very definite and distinct call from Jehovah, which made him the original and ideal highpriest (cf. Ex. 28:1). It was therefore felt that the Aaronic priesthood was supreme and final. But the Temple now lay in ruins, and the Aaronic priesthood no longer functioned. How then could Israel maintain his place in the favor of Jehovah? Why should the Messiah have tarried his return, and permitted such a catastrophe? Such questions would most naturally disturb a Christian Jew at about 85 to 90 A. D. This problem was the most difficult for the author to meet, but he attacks it courageously and with convincing proofs.

In meeting this problem the heart of his argument is that a subsequent appointment has superseded that of Aaron, and this superior appointment rested upon Jesus as the Messiah. He did not assume the glory of this office for himself, but in one Psalm (2:7) he is declared to be the Son of God, and in another (110:4) he is appointed to a higher order of priesthood than that of Aaron. This makes him transcend by far the Aaronic appointment.

The author has thrust forth three points which need proof. In the first place he has predicated the assumption that the Messiah has made himself subject to divine appointment and became obedient to divine authority. This is implied in the idea of Sonship —and much more strongly implied for the Jewish mind than for ours. To the Jew the position of son necessarily and inevitably involved subordination. Having accepted this status in the interrelations of divinity, Christ was in a position to receive appointment as highpriest. It was because God had declared of him, "Thou art my Son, I have this day begotten thee", that he was able to accept divine appointment. This status of Sonship was the basal premise. The appointment was conferred when the Holy Spirit declared through the Psalmist, "Thou art a priest."

The second point is that Christ as highpriest occupies a new order of priesthood, for it is said of him, "Thou art a priest after the order of Melchizedek".

Thirdly, the Melchizedek priesthood is final and eternal, for it is said of him, "Thou art a priest forever".

Thus we see that our author is following his distinctive custom of basing an elaborate argument upon a scripture predicate. Here he analyzes his scriptural basis by implication as follows: (i) "Thou art a priest"; (ii) "Thou art a priest after the order of Melchizedek"; (iii) "Thou art a priest forever".

(i) First we are shown that Christ accepted his appointment to the priesthood by manifest submission (5:7-10). Nothing could more convincingly present this attitude that the Gethsemane experience. Here Christ demonsrated beyond peradvenure his submission to the divine will. And the point of the author here is certainly well taken, for it was unquestionably in the Gethsemane experience that our Lord fought the battle with his natural human reluctance, and as the incarnate Son yielded by a voluntary act of his will to his priestly function in the atoning sacrifice of the cross. "Even though he was the Son, he learned obedience by the things which he suffered" (v. 8). That is, he laid aside the intrinsic harmony with the divine will which he possessed as the Second Person of the eternal Trinity, and came to the altar of surrender as a human, with all the inevitable struggle involved in human nature. It was in a distinctive sense the human Jesus who, in the shadows of Gethsemane, brought himself to say, "Thy will be done", and thereby opened the way to the altar of full surrender for all who would follow him.

(*ii*) Next the author grapples with the most difficult point of his entire discussion, the fact that the Melchizedek priesthood is superior to and therefore supersedes the Aaronic. The readers would not hesitate at all at the assumption that the Messiah was to fulfill the promised Melchizedek priesthood, nor that Jesus was the Messiah, but could any priesthood ever displace the sacred priesthood of Aaron? To establish this contention would require some subtle reasoning. Were his readers capable of comprehending it?

This last question is the occasion of the long parenthesis we have in 5:11-6:20. The comparative exhibition of the essential qualities of priesthood in Melchizedek and Christ is a profound process of reasoning to which the arrested spiritual progress of the readers presents an embarassing difficulty.

There is not in the epistle a more vivid reflection of the condition and reaction of the readers than we have in 5:11-6:3. They had been Christian believers for a long period. This harmonizes with the late date of the book. Some of them had known the gospel message from early youth. This extended period of experience and instruction should have qualified them to be teachers; but, on the contrary, they were exhibiting a need of instruction themselves. They showed shocking deficiency even in the most rudimentary elements of Christian truth. There was confusion and bewilderment about the things which they should have learned in the catechumenal stage of their Christian experience, and evidence of a tragic spiritual decadence. They had "*become* such as have need of milk" (v. 12). In former years there had been evidence of growth in knowledge and grace, but of late they had manifested a spiritual decline which their leader here described as a return to babyhood. "In effect, they are represented as in their dotage . . . They are not merely children, but in their second childhood" (A. B. Bruce, *The Ep. to the Heb.*, p. 197).

Verses 1 and 2 of the sixth chapter are especially illuminating in the light which they throw on the background of the epistle. (Cf. David Smith, *Disciple's Commentary,* in loco.) They may be translated thus: "Wherefore, leaving off the discussion of the origin of the Messiah, let us proceed to more mature matters, not laying again a foundation of repentance from dead works, and of faith in God, a teaching about washings and laying on of hands, of resurrection from the dead and final judgment." From these verses one can vividly picture what was being discussed in this Jewish Christian congregation, and the causes of alarm which were agitating them.

They had become disturbed about the question of "the origin of the Messiah." The Greek here literally means, "the beginning of the Christ", and very inadequately supports the ordinary rendering, "the first principles of Christ". The word Christ in Greek is a translation of Messiah in Hebrew or Aramaic. It appears here with the article, and consequently we render it "the Messiah". What the writer requests that they desist from is "the discussion of the origin of the Messiah". Then we conclude that the problem which was agitating these Jewish Christians was the origin of the Messiah: whence he should come and what should properly attest the beginning of his Messianic reign on earth—the old Pharisaic demand for a "sign". Had Jesus really fulfilled the proper role for the Messiah of Israel? Was it possible that they had been mistaken in accepting as their Messiah one who had become the Redeemer-god of a Gentile religion?

That much debated question of Jewish Christianity relative to faith and works had been revived, though in no way historically related to that which had called forth the corrective dissertations of Paul and James in former years. However, it was similar to the Pauline problem, for it was a dispute as to whether or not a Gentile might properly renounce the "dead works" of his blundering heathen efforts at religion, and properly manifest "faith in God" as the true object of worship, without becoming first a proselyte to Judaism. Were they not, in the eyes of Jehovah, contaminated by their contact with uncircumcised Gentiles?

As Christiains they had been led to lagely ignore all rules of ceremonial purity, so important to the devout Jew. Anxiety had begun to grip the consciences of some relative to the abandonment of these ceremonial ablutions, so they were seeking to renew a "teaching about washings". The word for "washings" is in the plural, and is not the Greek word commonly applied to Christian baptism. It is only by a strained and tedious interpretation that it can be construed as denoting the Christian ordinance. (Cf. Bruce, *op. cit.*, p. 205.) It becomes easy and natural when applied to Jewish ceremonies of purification, and understood as a problem disturbing Christian Jews—the question of Levitical purity.

Furthermore, could they be sure they had authorized teachers, when their teachers had never received "laying on of hands" from the rabbis in the synagogue? This is not the laying on of hands as a symbolic act accompanying the enduement of the Holy Spirit, but the ceremonial sign of sanction and conferring of authority in formal ordination to religious office. For a teacher of the Jews to be properly qualified required the imposition of hands by the older rabbis. The ever acute question of proper ordination of religious leadership, with its consequent right and prerogative, was being raised in this Jewish Christian congregation.

The final consummation toward which the religion of Jesus now seemed to be moving was very far from their original Jewish hopes. How could the Christian religion, as it was now developing, bring that "resurrection from the dead" of the elect of Israel and "final judgment" of the Gentile world which the Jew believed must mark the culmination of Messiah's reign? Yea verily, it seemed to be moving as rapidly as possible in the opposite direction! At A. D. 85 the Christian religion offered but faint hope of the realization of typically Jewish eschatological anticipations. It is easy to see how this fact might distress the heart of a Christian Jew.

Such must have been the questions which were dividing and perplexing this congregation of Hebrew Christians.

The reason for the obscurity which has veiled this passage from the understanding of interpreters has been the presumption that it was a comprehensive summary of rudimentary Christian teaching, and this misleading presumption has been based upon the erroneous translations of the Greek word *arches* (ἀρχῆς) in the first verse as "first principles". The confusion resulting from this approach is recognized by Bruce when he says, "What first strikes one in this primitive 'sum of saving knowledge' is how little that is specifically Christian it contains" (*op. cit.*, p. 200). We submit that it was not designed to present that which was "specifically Christian," but problems of Jewish religious faith and practice in the light of Christian teaching near the end of the first century. These strange-sounding phrases were topics of dispute and speculation in a Jewish Christian congregation which was growing wary of the innovations of a Messianic movement that was becoming more Gentile than Jewish.

The writer had determined to proceed with more advanced teaching (v. 3), for the simple reason that to take up anew these rudimentary questions with one who had already been saved would be wasted effort, for in case such an one had fallen away, it would be impossible for him to renew his beginning in the religion of Jesus, seeing that he had repudiated Jesus as Savior and abandoned his only hope of redemption. When we bear in mind the situation among these readers we recognize that what threatened them was not mere "backsliding", but a return to Judaism as a necessary element in salvation. It was impossible for them to go back and make a new beginning in Judaism, seeking to base there more thoroughly the fundamentals of religious experience, for in so doing they would be rejecting the only possible means of rdemption.

The English rendering in the American Standard Version implies that some of the readers had actually committed such apostasy, but the Greek does not require such a rendering, and the context of the epistle makes it abundantly clear that the readers had not actually abandoned and repudiated Christ. The verbs rendered in the A. S. V. as finite verbs are as a matter of fact participles, and do not require the idea that such apostacy had actually occurred. A more literal rendering, and one in far better accord with the context, would be: "For it would be impossible for those who were once enlightened by having tasted of the heavenly gift, and by having become partakers of the Holy Spirit, and by having tasted of the good word of God and the powers of the world to come, and having fallen away, to return afresh to repentance, for they would have crucified again upon their own responsibility the Son of God and held him up as a spectacle for ridicule." Hence the Greek admits of these verses being viewed as a hypothetical premise, used as a means of argument, and such an interpretation the context strongly demands. The author of Hebrews is not laying an oracular predicate for the theory of possible apostacy, but is seeking to enforce a strong warning to his confused and wavering readers. In verse 9 the author emphatically declares that he has really no fear that his readers will commit apostacy, but has confidence in their attainment of better things and things which, literally, "have a hold of salvation"; that is, things which are in harmony with the necessary nature of salvation.

This truth is enforced with an illustration from nature (vs. 7, 8). "For when the land drinks in the rain which comes frequently upon it, and bears vegetation which is of use to those in whose interest it has been tilled, it shares in blessings from God; but when it bears thorns and thistles, it is worthless and its cursing is at hand, it being finally destroyed by fire." If the readers will prove themselves to be genuine products of grace, bearing the characteristic fruit, they will receive the divine favor; but if they are manifestly a spurious growth, it is inevitable that they shall be discarded. The dominant note of this entire warning is, Without Christ you are left to utter desolation and hopelessness.

In the remainder of this parenthesis the writer turns the brighter side of the picture. His seemingly harsh warning has been given in the tenderness of a confident love, for he still believes in them and in their true salvation. A noble past of benevolent service, wherein they "ministered unto the saints, and still do minister," pleads effectively their cause with God. He is only concerned that their present diligence be commensurate with their past faithfulness.

Their hope as heirs of the covenant-promise to Abraham is based upon two means of divine security. The "two immutable things in which it is impossible for God to lie" are generally regarded as God's promise and God's oath. This is a natural inference from the English text, but the Greek word rendered "interposed" (ASV margin, "mediated") should correctly be rendered "pledged". Verses 17 to 19 may be read, "In such a manner God, willing to show more abundantly to the heirs of the covenant-promise the irrevocability of His counsel, made a *pledge* with an *oath,* in order that by two irrevocable things, in which it is impossible that God should lie, a strong encouragement might we have, who find our refuge by persistently clinging to the hope which lies before us, which we have as an anchor of the soul, both secure and dependable, and penetrating even to the solemn precincts of the Holy of Holies." The promise referred to in this connection is the covenant-promise made to Abraham, and it was this promise which God made doubly sure "by two irrevocable things". Then since it was the promise He was seeking to make sure, the promise could not be one of the things with which He made it sure. It would not be consistent to speak of securing the promise with the promise. He made doubly secure His covenant-promise because "He made a pledge with an oath". So God's pledge and God's oath were the two irrevocable things. God could not revoke His pledge, and of course could not revoke His pledge when secured by an oath. In the Greek text, in emphasizing the irrevocability of this twofold security of the believer, the author stresses by a device of the language (absence of the article) the character of God—"in which it is impossible for one who is *God* to lie". So great is this security that it is like an anchor of the soul made fast in heaven's innermost sanctuary. One "entering into the interior of the veil" in the Temple would penetrate to the Holy of Holies. It is in this Holy of Holies in heaven that Jesus officiates as our highpriest, "after the order of Melchizedek".

The writer has now returned with admirable ease to his original subject of the Melchizedek priesthood. Here it is necessary to convince his readers of two facts.

a. His argument from the Melchizedek priesthood is based upon the premise that it has its fulfillment in Christ. First of all his premise must be substantiated (7:1-3). This he does by showing certain points of similarity which were exceedingly forceful to his readers, but will be lost upon the twentieth century student unless he succeeds in entering into full sympathy with the first century Jew. The American revisers make the mistake of placing the chief point of the paragraph in brackets. Here (vs. 2, 3) the writer shows that the name and origin of Melchizedek foreshadowed the Christ. His Hebrew name meant "king of righteousness" (*melek*, king, and *zedek*, righteousness). The Hebrew word *shalem* meant peace; hence king of Salem meant king of peace. Jewish Christian readers would appreciate the point that these are two of the prominent characteristics of the Messiah of prophesy. It was also regarded as significant, and had been much discussed among Alexandrian Jews, that the record was absolutely silent with reference to the genealogy of Melchizedek, no mention whatever being made of his mother or father. To the Jew, with whom the matter of genealogy was so important in the case of any prominent leader, and especially if he were a priest, the absence of any genealogical indications in the record of Melchizedek was startling and highly significant. Neither is there any mention of his appointment as priest, nor the termination of his priesthood.

All these matters are wrapped in the veil of divine mystery, and the very mystery surrounding Melchizedek made him an object of great wonder and importance to the later Jewish mind. His priesthood became conceived as belonging to a transcendent and eternal order. In identifying it with the priesthood of Christ, the author thereby lifts Christ far above the Aaronic priesthood. The readers would be naturally inclined to accept the Messianic import of the Psalm quoted (110:4), so that the argument given here would serve to confirm them in that view. Jesus, their Messiah, was indeed the eternal priest of the Melchizedek order.

b. The most difficult fact for his readers to comprehend yet remained for the author to demonstrate. Was it possible that another priesthood could supersede the sacred priesthood of Aaron? This the author proves by one of his most forceful arguments, if looked at from the viewpoint of the Jewish mind (7:4-10).

He introduces the question by exclaiming, "Now consider how great this man was!" He was so great that Abraham, the father of all Israel, paid tithes to him. This was Abraham's own confession of subordination. Tithes were only paid by the less to the greater. The people paid tithes to the Levites, the Levites to the priests. Of course the priests as well as the Levites belonged to the tribe of Levi. Aaron himself was a child of Levi. But through Abraham Levi paid tithes to Melchizedek. Paying tithes was an act of homage, and homage was a confession of subordination. Thus the

Levitical priesthood, as descending from Abraham, was in a subordinate position to the Melchizedek priesthood.

Furthermore, Melchizedek blessed Abraham. In accordance with Hebrew custom, one acknowledged the superiority of another when he accepted from the other the formal act of blessing. The conception was logical. There would be no point to a blessing from an equal, and less from an inferior. "The less is blessed of the greater" (v. 7). This was an axiomatic rule in Jewish life and thought. Thus in another way Abraham acknowledged his inferiority to Melchizedek.

There was yet another point of transcendence in the Melchizedek priesthood. "And here men that die receive tithes; but there he receiveth them of whom it is witnessed that he liveth" (v. 8). The word "liveth" is in the present tense in the Greek, and might better be rendered, "liveth continually". The Aaronic priesthood is mortal; that of Melchizedek is defined by divine inspiration as immortal, for the scriptures never record his death. This argument from silence had great weight with the rabbinically trained Jewish mind.

This array of implications would be exceedingly impressive to Jewish Christian consciousness of the first century. In the face of it the Christian Jew must acknowledge the superiority of Melchizedek over Abraham. Then since Jesus was a priest "after the order of Melchizedek", as proven in 7:1-3, he was superior to the order of priesthood descended from Abraham.

Had the writer of Hebrew been employing modern devices of literary expression, he might have summarized his argument about as follows.

The comparison of the Messiahship of Jesus with the Melchizedek priesthood reveals two important facts.

A. The Messiahship of Jesus fulfills the Melchizedek priesthood, because Melchizedek presents three qualities which are unquestionably Messianic, and can only be fulfilled in the Messiah.

  a. He was king of righteousness.
  b. He was king of peace.
  c. He was independent of priestly lineage.

B. The priesthood of Jesus as fulfilling the Melchizedek priesthood supersedes that of Aaron at three points.

  a. It received tithes of the Aaronic priesthood.
  b. It blessed the Aaronic priesthood.
  c. It was immortal, while the Aaronic priesthood was mortal.

The conclusion is obvious. The Melchizedek priesthood of Jesus was designed to displace the priesthood of Aaron.

(*iii*) The third point of superiority in the divine appointment of Christ was his appointment to a more permanent office (7:11-25). He had been made "a priest forever". This finality of the Melchizedek priesthood of Jesus is proven by three arguments.

a. It involves a change in the Law, which means that the Aaronic priesthood cannot be regarded as permanent (vs. 11-19). Since the Law is "inextricably bound up with the Levitical priesthood" (Narborough, *Clarendon Bible* on Hebrews, p. 60), a change in the priesthood could not be made without a change in the Law. The scriptural promise of a new priesthood which should abide forever is proof positive that the Levitical priesthood was not designed to be permanent. Then in the very nature of the case there is required a change in the application of the Law, for the Law prescribes that a priest should be of the tribe of Levi, while Jesus, not a Levite, but of the tribe of Judah, has been proven to be the one who fulfills the Melchizedek priesthood. This is incontrovertible proof that the Mosaic code cannot be regarded as final, but must give place to a higher and eternal order even in the vital matter of priesthood.

b. The Melchizedek priesthood of Jesus has been established by a divine oath, which cannot be said of the priesthood of Aaron. "And by so much as it is not without an oath—for these have become priests without an oath, but he with an oath, through the authority of the one saying to him, The Lord *swore*, and shall not repent, Thou art a priest forever—by that much also Jesus has become security of a better covenant" (vs. 20, 21). The matter of an oath was intensely sacred to the Jewish mind, so that this argument had an appeal to those first readers which we are unable to appreciate.

c. The greater permanence of the priesthood of Jesus is to be seen in a comparison of the essential nature of the two priesthoods. "And they indeed have been made priests many in number, because that by death they are hindered from continuing: but he, because he abideth forever, hath his priesthood unchangeable" (vs. 23, 24). The priesthood established by the Mosaic Law has been rightfully set aside, for Levitical priests are but perishing mortals, while Christ as an infinite being has an unchangeable priesthood. Therefore his priestly ministry is abiding and final, as a consequence of which "he is able to save unto every frontier of experience those who seek to approach God through him, because he ever liveth to make intercession for them" (v. 25). Finality and sufficiency could not be more eloquently declared.

(2) *In Character*, 7:26-8:5. Having satisfactorily proven Christ's superiority in qualifications, the writer next proceeds to a summary of his superiority in character as a highpriest. It is summed up in two main characteristics.

i. The sort of highpriest who could properly fit the believer's need was *sinless* (7:26-28). "For indeed, this is the sort of highpriest who was adapted to us: holy, devoid of evil intent, stainless, in a class distinct from sinners, and having become exalted above the heavens" (v. 26). Such a highpriest was the one adapted or adequate for a redeemed race. "The new covenant is of no less moment than the old: a great salvation fitted for great purposes" (Mitchell, *Westminster N. T.*

on Heb. and Gen. Epp., p. 112). It was not required of him to offer up any sacrifices for his own sin; therefore he could offer sacrifices for the sins of the people, which he did with finality in the offering of himself. The priesthood of the Mosaic code was a faulty human priesthood, with all the infirmities of human nature. Therefore, the Aaronic highpriest must offer sacrifices for himself as well as for the people. Far superior was the priesthood of Christ, for as the Son of God he was eternally perfect.

ii. But in all these matters concerning the priesthood of Christ, the chief point is that he was *divine* (8:1-5). "Supreme, then, over the things which have been said: we have the kind of highpriest who sat down on the right hand of the Throne of the Majesty in the heavens." Thus having been exalted to an equal place with God upon His throne, he performs his priestly ministry in heaven, the ultimate source of all that is real in the worship of God, the place of purely divine operations. The scene of his heavenly ministry is the real Tabernacle, of which all the facilities and functions of the earthly priesthood are but shadowy reflections. But Christ would of necessity be eliminated if the readers were bent upon the perpetuation of the Aaronic priesthood; for that was constituted by the Law, according to which a descendant of the tribe of Judah could have no part in the priestly ministrations. This Tabernacle ministry, however, was but a shadowy reproduction of the original pattern in heaven, as we may see in the divine instruction given to Moses that he make the Tabernacle according to the heavenly "pattern" which was revealed to him in the Mount. Thus Christ is the divine original, while the Aaronic priesthood is but a human reproduction in shadowy types, imperfect at best. Indeed, this is the chief point!

Let it be observed that the author of Hebrews does not repudiate the Aaronic priesthood as having been of merely human origin and without redemptive significance. He believes that it was designed and devised of God, but only as preparatory and typical, and ordained to be displaced by the original and final reality which consisted in the priesthood of Jesus. He is not pointing out its weaknesses to condemn it *per se*, but to show its inadequacy for eternal purposes. It was provisional; the priesthood of Christ is final.

(3) *In Ministry*, 8:6-10:18. Having pointed out the superiority of Christ to the Aaronic priesthood in qualifications and character, the writer now proceeds to establish the fact of his superiority in ministry.

There is a message of comfort here for the readers not only as Christians but as Jews. The Temple at Jerusalem lay in ruins; the priesthood had ceased to function; no highpriest entered the Holy Place on the Day of Atonement; sacrifices could never again be offered to Jehovah. To see in Jesus the complete and transcendent fulfillment of all this ministry was indeed a consolation. This ministry was (i) based upon the Abrahamic covenant; (ii) performed in the Tabernacle and the Temple; (iii) administered through the Levitical sacrifices. At all these points the writer shows that the ministry of Jesus is better.

i. It is based upon a *better covenant* (8:6-13). The covenant upon which the new ministry is based is a better covenant because it offers better promises: promises which are guaranteed of fulfillment. Once more the writer is found shocking tender Jewish sensibilities. "For if that first one had been faultless, then a place would not have been sought for a second" (v. 7). The startled Jewish Christian would wish to cry out, "What! The Abrahamic covenant imperfect and insecure!" Yes, for the scriptures themselves render such a verdict. But the author so puts the matter as to throw the blame fundamentally on Israel rather than God's covenant with Abraham. He does not say, "Finding fault with it", but, significantly, "Finding fault with *them*", and the gender of the Greek pronoun shows conclusively that it refers to the Israelites and not the promises. The fulfillment of the former promise had been conditioned upon the formal obedience of Israel to God's law. But the Israelites defaulted in their side of the covenant. Jehovah declares that it failed "because they did not continue on in my covenant" (v. 9). So God provided a new covenant, in which the promises were based upon a spiritual transformation in the hearts of the people, which spiritual transformation God Himself would accomplish. God proposed to assume both sides of the contract! Consequently, there is not any question about it being carried out.

However grievous it may appear to the devout

Jew, this inevitably means the passing of the old order. "When he says *new*, he makes the first old; so that which is growing old and becoming decrepit is near the vanishing point" (v. 13). Jerusalem lay in ruins, the Temple was a heap of debris, the sacrifices had ceased, the Gentile conqueror held the Land in tyrannical grip, and Israel was scattered to the four corners of the earth: indeed the Abrahamic regime *was* at the vanishing point!

ii. The new ministry was performed through a *better service* (9:1-22). Where the word *covenant* occurs in the first verse it is supplied by the translators, and does not have a corresponding word in the original. We believe that the word *ministry* should be supplied instead, for when the course of the argument is studied closely we discern that the author is here presenting another proof that Christ has "obtaind a more excellent ministry" (8:6) than that of the old order. The comparison here is between the old and new ministry, so we would render the first verse, "Now again, the first ministry had also ceremonies of worship and its sanctuary of this world."

The first ministry, that of the Tabernacle, was necessarily transient because composed of transitory and perishable elements. This passage suggests a revival of interest in the Tabernacle service, and there are evidences from other sources that such a revival came in the last quarter of the first century. Reference to the Tabernacle would be of special force to Hellenistic Jews, who had been separated from the Temple worship, and had consequently higher regard for the historical Tabernacle service than did the Palestinian Jews. This fact would be intensified by the destruction of the Temple at Jerusalem.

(*i*) The transient ministry prescribed for the Tabernacle consisted of external rites, and did not affect the inner and spiritual life of the individual; could not, "as touching the conscience, make the worshipper perfect" (9:1-10).

(*ii*) The ministry of Christ possesses greater efficacy because it does not depend upon material elements, and can achieve internal and spiritual results (9:11-22). His death has made effective the new covenant, even as death makes effective a will (the word for will and covenant is the same in the Greek). His death on the cross also fulfilled the requirement that there should be shedding of blood for remission.

We find presented in these verses (9:1-22) a very clear contrast between the old ministry and the new. There are four points in this antithetical comparison.

(*a*) The first ministry is performed through an earthly service: "Now then, the first ministry had also ceremonies of worship and its sanctuary *of this world*" (v. 1). The second ministry is performed through a heavenly service: "On the other hand Christ, as he appears in comparison, is a highpriest of the good things that are to come, through the greater and more perfect tabernacle not made with hands; that is, *not of this creation*" (v. 11).

(b) The first ministry is provided with a man-made equipment (vs. 2-5). "For there was a Tabernacle constructed" (v. 2). The writer closes his description of the material furnishings of the Tabernacle with the remark, "Concerning which things we have no occasion to speak in detail" (v. 5). Hence his purpose is not a detailed description of the sanctuary, but to call attention to its material composition. It "was constructed." The second ministry is provided with an equipment "not made with the hands" (v. 11).

(c) The first ministry could only produce external effects (vs. 6-9). The way into the actual holy presence of God cannot be revealed "while the first Tabernacle yet has standing" (v. 8). The Holy Spirit is here regarded as the divine author of the Tabernacle, and as teaching through it that the way to the holy presence of God is closed so long as the Tabernacle of the first ministry holds its place of service, or "has standing." It cannot "as touching the conscience make the worshipper perfect" (v. 9). The second ministry is internal in its effects. It is able "to cleanse your conscience from dead works to serve the living God" (v 14).

(d) The first ministry is temporary in nature. It consists of "carnal regulations, set up pending a time of reconstruction" (v. 10). The second ministry is permanent in nature. It insures that "they that have been called may receive the promise of the eternal inheritance" (v. 17).

This comparison may be graphically presented thus:

The First Ministry	The Second Ministry
An earthly service— "of this world."	A heavenly service— "not of this creation."
Human equipment— "there was a tabernacle constructed."	Divine equipment— "not made with hands."
External effects— "cannot as touhcing the conscience make the worshipper perfect."	Internal effects— "cleanse your conscience from dead works to serve the living God."
Temporary in nature— "carnal regulations set up pending a time of reconstruction."	Permanent in nature— "the promise of the eternal inheritance."

This comparison could be worked out in even greater detail, but we must avoid fanciful extremes. May it also be observed that the first century Jewish author of Hebrews had no such definite analysis in mind, though we may legitimately summarize in this form for our own convenience the points of comparison which appear in his discussion.

iii. The priestly ministry of Christ is better than that of the old order because it is accomplished by a *better sacrifice* (9:23-10:18). The sacrifice of Christ is superior to the Levitical sacrifice by reason of its immediate and final effectiveness. It is thus effective for two reasons.

(i) It was made in the real, immediate presence of God (9:24). It was not in a sanctuary prepared merely as a type to symbolize the heavenly reality that Christ entered, but into the real heavenly sanctuary itself, to offer his sacrifice in the very presence of God.

(ii) It was offered once for all (9:25-10:18). The Levitical sacrifices were offered daily, and the sacrifice of the Atonement was offered annually; but not so with the sacrifice of Christ. He was not crucified again and again, but in keeping with the essential course of human experience he died once, for "it is appointed unto men once to die, then after this, judgment" (v. 27). And when he returns for the consummation of his redemptive work it will not be to die again, for he shall appear next time "apart from sin" (v. 28), to receive unto himself those who wait in faith for his salvation.

The very provision made by the Law is *prima facie* evidence that its sacrifices are not finally effective (10:1-4). The Law only holds a shadowy type of those blessed realities which are reserved for the redeemd, and therefore cannot be final. It provides for a recurrence of the sacrifices, "year by year" (v. 1), which shows that at no time can they accomplish a perfect work. They leave the worshipper still under the dark shadow of the consciousness of sin. The author sums up this obvious insufficiency of the recurrent Levitical sacrifices in the fourth verse, placing special stress upon the impossibility of their final efficacy. *"Impos-*

sible then for the blood of bulls and goats to take away sin."

Not so with the sacrifice of Christ (10:5-18). In his atoning ministry we are to discern two fundamental and climactic implications. (*a*) It was not in the plan of God to make the Levitical sacrifices final, but to bring in another sacrifice more satisfactory to His divine will (vs. 5-9). This he proves by a striking quotation from the fortieth Psalm, which contains two significant statements, "Sacrifices and offerings and whole burnt offerings and sacrifices for sin thou wouldst not, neither hast pleasure therein," and, "Lo, I am come to do thy will." The former sacrifice did not fulfill perfectly the divine will, so Christ came for such a perfect fulfillment. "He taketh away the first that he may establish the second" (v. 9). Since God was not entirely pleased with the old sacrifice, it may readily be seen that He would displace it with something better and final. (b) The second fundamental implication is that the fact that the sacrifice of Christ was offered only once indicates that a perfect work of cleansing was then accomplished (vs. 10-18). The chief point of the passage is in verse 14, "For by one offering he has perfected forever those who are being sanctified." This final sufficiency of the sacrifice of Christ is attested by divine inspiration. "Jeremiah's ideal of a true religion is again quoted, and the last line, 'their sins will I remember no more,' leads up to the triumphant conclusion of the writer's long argument . . . For 'remembering sins no more' means that they are really taken away. The real remission of sins which is taking place amongst those who are leading the consecrated life looking unto Jesus, is an experienced fact which shows that there is no need of further offering for sin. The new covenant is made, signed, sealed, accepted" (Mitchell, *op. cit.*, p. 133).

APPLICATION, 10:19-13:17

In the remaining chapters of the epistle the author makes a practical application of what has preceded, and delineates the Christian graces consequent upon the superiority of Christ. Four such graces are presented: courage, faith, fortitude, and holiness.

Courage, 10:19-38

The minds of these Hebrew Christians had become confused. The widening breach between Christianity and Judaism had frightened them. They had now assumed a rather vacillating attitude, scarcely knowing whether to cling to Christianity or go back to Judaism, or at least to seek a merger of the two. Recognizing this wavering state of mind, the writer seeks to inspire new courage. The three paragraphs of this section indicate the three means he employs. First he uses a word of exhortation, then a word of warning, and finally a word of reminder.

(1) *A Word of Exhortation,* 10:19-25. Some of the readers had grown negligent in their Christian duty, and were losing the fervor of their Christian spirit. As the author earnestly admonishes them he

builds his exhortation around three dominant notes, "let us draw near" (v. 22), "let us hold fast" (v. 23), and "let us consider one another" (v. 24). That is, their discouragement threatened them with spiritual decline along three lines, communion with God, confidence in the truth, and earnest Christian service. All three are exceedingly vital points in Christian experience. It is interesting to note that the author regards as an essential part of their Christian service the "assembling together" for worship. One of the first duties which discouragement had caused the readers to neglect was attendance upon public worship.

(2) *A Word of Warning*, 10:26-31. The author next warns them against the risk of renouncing Christianity. If the repudiation of Moses, who was merely a servant of God, meant death, what must be the consequences of the repudiation of God's own Son! Since Christ is God's only appointed way of approach for sinful man, it inevitably means spiritual disaster to reject that way. This passage has no connection with the idea of apostacy as debated in modern Protestant Christianity, but is an emphatic pronouncement upon the sufficiency of Christ alone for salvation. It is Christ or doom.

(3) *A Word of Reminder*, 10:32-38. We have in this paragraph an appeal upon the basis of former faithfulness. They had recently passed through an experience of severe persecution, and had rmained loyal to Christ and his cause. As they endured patiently the

ill-treatment by their enemies during that period of stress, so the author now urges that they manifest a like courage in the face of the present crisis. Whether the crisis which now confronted them was a general persecution, it would not be possible to say in the light of this passage alone. However, the comparison of this passage with 12:1-3 makes the theory of a general persecution plausible. The previous persecution, in which the readers had shown marked faithfulness, was most probably the Neronian persecution, while the one now threatening can best be thought of as the Domitianic persecution. Such a theory is helpful, though not indispensible, in interpreting these passages.

Faith, 10:39-11:40

A phrase in the Old Testament quotation used in the preceding passage suggested the idea of faith, so the author proceeds to its discussion. We do not have here the characteristic Pauline conception of faith. There are three aspects of faith presented in the New Testament: (1) self-committal for salvation; (2) affectionate trustfulness; (3) obedient allegiance to Christ. Paul emphasizes the first, while the author of Hebrews emphasizes the third. It is faithful allegiance to Christ for which he is appealing.

The author shows what such allegiance has wrought in the history of Israel. He sets forth this catalogue of Israei's heroes to prove two points, which are introduced in 11:1. In this verse "the object of the writer is not to give a formal definition of Faith but to bring out characeristics of Faith which bear upon his argument" (Westcott, *Hebrews*, in loco). The word rendered "substance" in the old version and "assurance" in the revised, should doubtless best be rendered "realization." "Faith is realization of things hoped for." Faith brings to reality things which are hoped for—but not always. Sometimes hope fails to reach its fruition in this earthly existence. Then faith becomes the "proof" of things which are never really seen. The author gives from Israel's history the concrete cases which demonstrate this twofold function of faith. "For in such a faith as this the elders have been offered as testimony" (v. 2). So there are two fundamental facts about faith which the heroes of Israel's past are brought forward to prove.

(1) That the greatest achievements in their history had been accomplished through faith (11:3-12). The very initial revelation of the scriptures, the creation of the world, could only have been received through faith, since no witness could have left the record thereof. It was by faith that Abel surpassed Cain in the favor of God; by faith Enoch attained to his transcendent place in history; by faith Noah achieved the salvation of his family in the time of the Flood; by faith Abraham received his heritage and produced his divinely appointed progeny. These were the preëminent facts of the past, and were all based upon faith.

(2) That these heroes persisted in their faith and allegiance to God in spite of the fact that they did not in this world realize the perfect fruition of their

hopes (11:13-40). All these accomplishments by the saints of old looked forward to a redeemed society, under the reign of the Messiah of promise. This ultimate realization they never received, but persevered in faith. Doubtless the Hebrew Christian readers of this epistle had been growing impatient for some fulfillment of hope which had not yet been realized. This was in all probability the Second Coming of Christ. The Messiah had not returned, and, confused as they already were, their unrest was aggravated by the fear that their waiting might be in vain. Their anti-Christian Jewish neighbors would not lose the opportunity of chiding them for the disappointment of their hope. In 11:13-40 the author shows them that all such matters must submissively yield to the larger plan of God.

Fortitude, 12:1-13

It is clear from this passage that the Hebrew Christians were either in the midst of a severe persecution, or, more probably, threatened with one. It is altogether possible that this was a local difficulty, but a comparison of this passage with 10:32-34 fits strikingly into the Neronian persecution of 64-67, and that under Domitian 85-96. The passage before us appeals for Christian fortitude in the face of persecution which threatens, and urges the adequate motives for such fortitude. Three are presented.

(1) *The Heritage of Sacrificial Faith*, 12:1. This looks back at the preceding chapter. The cloud of witnesses with which the readers are compassed are the

heroes of faith which have been exhibited above. And the word rendered "witnesses" does not mean merely spectators, but those who can bear witness of what the anticipated race should be. They are themselves veterans of the race-course. The challenge and inspiration of these onlooking veterans should move the Christian to offer his best. In order to attain his best on the Christian race-course he must do two things. (*i*) He must "lay aside every weight." This likely looks at the doubt and worry with which the readers had allowed themselves to be burdened down. (*ii*) He must discard "the sin which so easily hinders." With these readers doubtless the most alluring sin was looking with envy and longing toward the old traditions and ceremonies of Judaism which they had abandoned when they espoused the Christian religion. Removing these hindrances they are to run with fortitude the Christian race.

(2) *The Example of Jesus,* 12:2, 3. The readers are admonished to "look away yonder unto Jesus," who is far above and far ahead of them in every conceivable respect. He is both the author and finisher of faith: he originated it and he consummated it. But to reach his exalted state he walked unfalteringly to the cross, and hesitated not at the shame which was heaped upon him. The readers had known no such suffering and no such embarassment as he was forced to endure.

(3) *Their Relation to God,* 12:4-13. Their burden of trial was relatively light as compared with some,

who had been called upon to shed their blood and even give their lives for the faith; and, after all, as sons of God they should expect chastening. Such their scriptures taught them. This chastening, however, was not the vindictive punishment of aliens, but the loving discipline of children, even as earthly parents in love disciplined their offspring. This discipline of distress, grievous for the moment, would, if patiently endured, eventually bear its blessed fruit.

Holiness, 12:14-13:17

The corruption and dissipation of the first century world were shockingly excessive, and the Jews, even Jewish Christians, were not unaffected by it. And there is "nothing more injurious to a Christian community than controversy and the embitterment which it breeds" (David Smith, *Commentary,* in loco), so the readers of this epistle, because of their confusion and misunderstanding, were in unusual moral jeopardy. So the author appropriately closes his discussion by reinforcing their moral resistance.

(1) *The Meaning of Holiness,* 12:14-17. The meaning of "sanctification" as used in this passage is undoubtedly connected with right living. The fundamental idea of the New Testament word is separation. Here it means separation in a moral sense. It is that purification of mind and heart "without which no man shall see the Lord." There is here an inescapable echo of the words of the Master, "Blessed are the pure in heart, for they shall see God" (Mt. 5:8). But it is clear

that the practical purpose of the author is to urge his readers to live separate from the excessive corruption of the world of that day. The question of sinless perfection is not contemplated, the point of emphasis being moral excellence, as may be seen from a study of the passage as a whole. It is not falling short of perfection which is contemplated, but falling short of the grace of God—failing to appropriate the grace of God in consistent living. It is the harvest of bitterness which the author fears, and the regrets of a hasty decision, made in the moment of passion or impatience, such as that of Esau, who, spurred by the pangs of physical hunger, blundered into a foolish bargain which cost him his birth-right. So our author is not laying down a rigid precept of sinlessness, but urging his readers to assert anew their moral vigor, by the grace of God, and not yield to temptations in the time of weakness which future regrets can never remedy.

(2) *The Incentive to Holiness,* 12:18-29. The incentive to holiness is the glorious goal or destiny of a redeemed life. The Christian is not approaching an objective of formal restrictions, such as obtained at Sinai, but a destination which calls for correct conduct and loyal faith by its transcendent nature. The crime of inconsistency is that the Christian is sinning against the holy destiny for which he is intended. There is thrilling dramatic progress in the author's description of this glorious destiny of the redeemed.

i. The spirit of the redeemed approaches not the horrors of Mt. Sinai, but the glories of Mt. Zion, where is that heavenly abiding place in which dwells the living God Himself. The beauty of the writer's language is only impaired by paraphrase, "the city of the living God, the heavenly Jerusalem" (v. 22).

ii. He comes "to innumerable hosts of angels," who are gathered in a general assembly as enrolled citizens of the heavenly city. The idea here is not of a "glory church," but of the angels as enrolled citizens in the heavenly *ekklesia*, assembly (vs. 22, 23).

iii. He comes to the great seat of divine justice, where the eternal Judge will take his case in hand, and avenge all the wrongs he has suffered (v. 23).

iv. He comes to the exultant band of the redeemed, who have preceeded him to the other side (v. 23).

v. He comes to Jesus! And he comes not to him as the executer of the Sinaitic covenant, but as the mediator of a new covenant. This covenant, like the old covenant, is confirmed by the sprinkling of blood, but blood which has a better story to tell than that of Abel! The Greek word here for speak means to converse or relate. If these Jewish Christians believe that the message which relates the story of the blood of Abel is divinely safeguarded, much more should they stand in awe before that message whose heart is the blood of the Son of God. If in the old revelation God's voice shook the very earth, the seismic impact of His power which He promised for the new revelation will be far more severe, and will leave only those things which have real eternal value. These things constitute a kingdom which shall stand forever, even in the face of God's testing power.

(3) *The Practice of Holiness*, 13:1-17. Here the author presents a few of the specific matters involved in holy living. There are four practical points suggested.

i. The writer exhorts his readers to manifest *an altruistic spirit* (vs. 1-3). Discouragement had a tendency to destroy their brotherly fellowship. This brotherly love was especially needed in two particulars. (*i*) In those days there were few hotel accomodations, and those traveling were largely dependent on the hospitality of friends or those in a common religious or fraternal group for food and shelter. This necessary service must not be neglected, especially in the light of its sanction in the experience of Abraham. (*ii*) Some of their brother Christians were suffering persecution, even to bonds; these must be comforted and cared for by those still in more fortunate state.

ii It is necessary to admonish even these Jewish Christians to *domestic integrity* (v. 4), for the severe temptations constantly thrust upon them by their environment and their own bewilderment laid them open to great moral risk.

iii. It is in line with the age long weakness of the Jew that the author deems it well to urge upon his readers *freedom from avarice* (vs. 5-7). Two incentives are offered, the admonition and assurance of their scriptures and the sacrifice of their martyred leaders. Among these martyred leaders, the "going forth" from whose careers the readers are admonished to remember, were Paul and Peter.

iv. Discouragement and confusion had made necessary the exhortation to *faithfulness in religious duties* (vs. 8-17). Since Christ remains unchangeable their faith should remain unchangeable, and not be disturbed by any taunts as to their belonging to a religion which ignored regulations relative to the eating of meats or was without any divinely established altar. When Jesus was sacrificed according to the divinely directed plan, "without the gate," he established an altar and a fellowship far superior to anything offered in the Tabernacle worship. Hence the Hebrew Christian should cease to pine for his former customs of worship, and remain loyal to the simple worship of the unchanging Christ.

Conclusion, 13:18-25

Here several personal matters are mentioned which are of great historical interest, and throw at least a little light on the origin of the epistle.

(1) It would seem that the author is absent from his people because of some involuntary restraint, probably being in prison or exile (vs. 18, 19). He is anxious that his life shall be known as in every respect honorable, which would suggest solicitude because of some reflection upon his reputation. Combining with

these suggestions his anxiety to be restored to them at the earliest possible moment and the evidences of the epistle that it was written under the menace of persecution, we would conclude that the author is suffering an enforced absence from his readers.

(2) It appears that the author was a close personal friend to Timothy, who also was known to his readers (v. 23). This is sometimes used as proof for the Pauline authorship, but the use of it really serves to prove the weakness of the theory, for one is taking an obviously extreme and strained position who assumes that Paul was the only one ever close to Timothy in the fellowship of Christian service. Of course a man of Timothy's qualities and influence had many close friends, before and after Paul's death. Timothy is in prison, and the writer is waiting near at hand until he has been released, which would strongly suggest Timothy's superiority to the writer. At least it is a little difficult to imagine Paul as lingering around waiting for Timothy to get out of prison, and especially as uncertain as to just whether Timothy will accompany him on his return, as the last clause of the verse suggests.

(3) It would appear from verse 24*a* that the epistle was not to a church at large, but to a congregation within a church, for the author would hardly send salutations to the elders if he knew the elders would be the first to receive the letter.

(4) It seems probable from verse 24*b* that this congregation resided in Italy, for the Greek of the

passage rendered literally reads, "Those from Italy salute you." It would appear then to refer to other prisoners or visitors from an Italian congregation who are present with the writer. If the congregation addressed resided in Italy, then it was most likely a Jewish congregation of the church at Rome. This inference finds corroboration in the fact that the earliest evidence we have of any use of this letter comes from the epistle of Clement of Rome, about A. D. 97.

Thus closes one of the towering peaks of redemptive revelation. Nowhere has the triumphant Christian spirit inscribed with more sublime or terrific force its unshakable confidence in the supremacy and finality of Jesus Christ as sufficient Savior and eternal Lord. To Him be the glory forever and ever! Amen.

ADDENDUM

REACTIONARY JEWISH CHRISTIANITY

From the standpoint of the Pauline gospel, which in essential substance became the doctrinal standard of the apostolic churches, we would describe the developments before us here as "heretical" Jewish Christianity, but to use the term "reactionary" is more in line with a purely historical treatment. It is undoubtedly well that Paul's teaching did prevail, and we believe it represented the correct redemptive revelation as given under the direction of the Holy Spirit, but the Pauline view was far from acceptable to the strictest element in Jewish Christianity—and they regarded him as "heretical."

By the dawn of the second century the more liberal elements of Jewish Christianity had been entirely absorbed by the Gentile churches: indeed, there were probably but a scattering few Jewish Christians in the Gentile churches at 100 A. D. The only distinct survival of Jewish Christianity which the second century witnessed was a much altered form of that reaction in the early apostolic churches which we are accustomed to designate as the Judaizing movement.

Detailed treatment of the Judaizers belongs to the life and literature of Paul, but brief notice is given of it here for sake of completeness in the discussion of Jewish Christianity. It was without question an abortive developement and subversive of the true spirit and concept of the religion of Jesus, but it was nevertheless historically a development of Jewish Christianity.

The ultimate origin of the Judaizing reaction must be traced back to the example and teaching of Jesus. Such an observation at first startles and offends evangelical Christian sensibilities, but mature consideration makes the fact quite obvious. It resulted from a misunderstanding and extreme application of the teaching and conduct of the Master. He was faithful in his discharge of the requirements of the Law, and declared it to be his unalterable purpose to fulfill the Law rather than destroy it, maintaining that it must be conserved in every jot (*yodh*) and tittle. However, at the same time he insistently urged that the Law should receive a spiritual and practical rather than a physical and mechanical application. It was this last point which the Judaizers utterly missed. They heartily accepted the Messiahship of Jesus, but saw him as exclusively a Jewish Messiah, who by precept and example had upheld the Law and traditions of Israel. As such a Messiah, the benefits of his mission could only accrue to those who were Jews or proselytes of Judaism.

A sympathetic and proper understanding of the spirit and message of Jesus condemns such a conclusion as a false deduction, but obviously it was an easy inference for the Jewish mind to draw. At the beginning of the Christian movement, immediately following Pentecost, this was the prevailing if not the unanimous view of the significance of Jesus' Messianic mission. Only gradually did the missionary spirit assert itself and the narrow exclusiveness of Judaism diminish in the Palestinian churches. And throughout the primitive history of the Christian movement there persisted a circle of Jewish disciples who regarded Jesus as the Messiah wholly and only of Judaism and its proselytes.

The persistence of this view was probably an effect upon the Christian movement exerted by Pharisaism. There were likely a few Pharisees among the primitive disciples, and certainly quite a number who had been deeply imbued with the Pharisaic spirit and teaching. To such it would be inconceivable that an unclean Gentile should share in the blessings of the Messianic kingdom. Jehovah's covenant was with Abraham and his seed, and only those lineally or ceremonially related to Abraham could inherit the promises. Upon this position the Pharisee would insist with unyielding tenacity. This attitude is basal and obvious in the Judaizing reaction. Hence the Judaizer must have been a Pharisee or follower of the Pharisees who had espoused the Messianic cause of Jesus.

To Jewish Christians of this fundamentally Pharisaic viewpoint there were two tendencies of Jewish Christianity which were objectionable.

(1) The first was the disposition of the disciples, especially those in Jerusalem, to treat the Hellenistic Jews as on an equality socially and religiously with the Jews of Palestine (cf. Ac. 6:1ff.). The Jew of the Gentile world was inescapably defiled by Gentile contacts. Besides, he could not maintain the unwavering loyalty to the Law and traditions of Israel which characterized the devout Jew of Palestine. In the es-

sential nature of the case the Hellenistic Jew could not be the true child of Abraham which his Palestinian brother could be. Consequently the Jew of Palestine was on a higher religious plane, and deserved greater consideration and superior privileges. For the Jerusalem church, and doubtless other Palestinian churches, to disregard this distinction created a deep offence for the more Pharisaic among the Jewish disciples. It was regarded as a policy of heretical compromise.

(2) The large majority of the early disciples were from the *am ha-'aretz*, or "country people," who had no great sympathy for or interest in the rigid views and demands of Pharisaism. They were therefore prepared to be more generously inclined toward the Gentile world and favorable toward offering the gospel to the Gentiles. It was this fact in the character of Palestinian Christianity which offered a foundation for the development of the missionary spirit, and made possible the spread of the redemptive message of Jesus to the Gentile world.

But there was in the early Jewish churches a strong counter tendency. When Peter took, with great caution and reserve, the first step toward the Gentile as an object of the gospel, there arose an insistent protest from the Pharisaic element (Ac. 11:2), and when the persecution provoked by the activities of Stephen sent many Hellenistic Jews out into the Gentile world with the gospel, and actually initiated the development of a Gentile church in Antioch, a very definite effort was made in Jerusalem to check the liberalizing tendency (Ac. 11:22).

The reaction was persistent but in vain. The gospel went to the Gentile, and the Jew was the herald of its good tidings. While Hellenistic Judaism was the chief means for the propagation of the Christian religion in the Graeco-Roman world, yet the source and incipiency were in Palestine, and were the occasion of a severe conflict. This agitation continued through a large part of Paul's experience, and constituted a large element in the background of his epistles.

Beyond the end of the first century Judaistic Christianity appears in only a few literary reflections, and occasional and rather prejudiced references by the early church fathers. It is quite clearly reflected in the fragments of the socalled "Gospel of the Hebrews," which was a Judaized revision of Matthew, written in Aramaic, and used by a Jewish Christian sect referred to by ancient writers as the "Nazarenes." This title is likely a survivial of the earliest designation of Christian Jews in Palestine by their contemporaries, and was still retained by Judaistic Christians into the second or third century. From the existing fragments of this apocryphal Gospel we would infer that the survivors of the Judaizing movement were still loyal to the Messiahship of Jesus, and to much of his practical teaching. The Nazarenes were never far from Pauline Christianity in essential doctrine, and survived to at least the fourth century.

The Gospel of the Hebrews forms our connecting link between the primitive Judaizing Christians and the second century Ebionites. The term "Ebonite" was applied to the primitive disciples because of their extreme and prevalent poverty. In the second century it came to be confined to Jewish Christians who repudiated Gentile Christianity and the teaching of Paul. They made considerable use of the Gospel of the Hebrews, and of what was doubtless a revision of that Gospel in the direction of more extreme anti-Paulinism, known as the "Gospel of the Ebionites." The Ebionite movement eventually divided into three branches: those who accepted the supernatural origin of Jesus, but not his universal Messiahship; those who denied the Virgin Birth as well as universal salvation; and those who subscribed to the theories of Gnosticism. On one point, however, they continued to agree—opposition to Paul and Gentile Christianity. The Ebionite movement seems to have extended as far as the fourth century.

By the end of the fourth century the last trace of distinctive Jewish Christianity had disappeared. The church at Jerusalem was dominantly if not exclusively Gentile, and the same was true of Palestinian Christianity as a whole. No trace is to be found of a distinctively Jewish Christian congregation anywhere in the world at 400 A. D. Israel had utterly eschewed the bonds of Christ, and groped away to the sad doom which he called down upon his own head when before Pilate's judgment seat he ruthlessly shouted, "His blood be upon us and our children!"

LITERATURE

Four works representative of the development in method of approach to the study of Jewish Christianity have already been mentioned in the Preface. Among them, that by Cartwright (*Hebrew Christian Church of Jerusalem*) is of value only as illustrating the prevailing viewpoint of a century ago. Appearing two years later (1844), but of more real value, is Lyman Coleman's work, *The Apostolical and Primitive Church*. The traditional viewpoint is preserved and thoroughly discussed in Vaughn, *The Church of the First Days*, a series of lectures on Acts. Dobschuetz, *Christian Life in the Primitive Church*, is definitely influenced by the traditional assumption that Jewish Christianity was practically confined to the brief view of it given in Acts, but a large section of the book is devoted to a valuable discussion of "Jewish Christendom" (Book II, pp. 138-172). Hunkin, *The Earliest Christian Church*, was published recently, and represents the traditional approach employed in the light of present day scholarship.

For a rigidly critical approach, and one which entirely abandons all doctrinal and traditional interest, there are four quite recent works which we may suggest. F. C. Grant's translation of Kundsin's "Primitive Christianity in the Light of Gospel Research" in his *Form Criticism* offers in a very brief scope the method of approach which holds supreme attention in the field of New Testament scholarship today. It treats early Christian life in the light of what is known as

Formgeschichte. Of the same intensely critical nature is Riddle, *Early Christian Life.* In the recently published work of Martin Dibelius, *A Fresh Approach to the New Testament and Early Christian Literature,* one may find the application of *Formgeschichte* to all the literary activity of Apostolic and sub-Apostolic times. Another recent work of interest is that by Lietzmann, *History of the Early Church,* which is a work abreast with the very latest methods of approach to early Christian history, and dealing rather largely with Jewish Christianity of the Apostolic Age.

The *Formgeschichte* method of historical approach is ably discussed by its pre-eminent apostle in the recent English edition of Dibelius' work, *From Tradition To Gospel.* As is evident from the title, this book deals primarily with Gospel sources, but in doing so treats much of first century Christian life and the Palestinian churches.

As to the book of Acts, we would suggest that the leading critical commentary is the work on Acts in five volumes which constitutes Part I of Foakes-Jackson and Lake, *The Beginnings of Christianity.* In this ponderous work every aspect of critical interpratation is thoroughly wrought out. The translation and commentary (vol. iv) are by Cadbury. Another splendid critical commentary on Acts may be found in Knowling's contribution to the *Expositor's Greek Testament.* Quite recently the great Lutheran scholar Lenski has published a great critical commentary, conserving largely the orthodox point of view, under the simple title, *The Acts of the Apostles.* Hackett's work, *A Commentary on the Original Text of the Acts of the Apostles,* is old and not abreast with up-to-date methods of critical exegesis, but contains much valuable material. He also wrote on Acts for the *American Commentary,* which is based upon the English text.

The author would acknowledge especially his own dependence upon Carver, *The Acts of the Apostles,* a splendid work which employs the English text in discussion but is based upon a long and careful investigation of the original. The average student will find this work exceedingly valuable. Surely one of the best expositions of this New Testament book, a commentary prepared for the English student, is to be found in Stifler on *The Acts of the Apostles.* It is relatively old, but still very useful. The student who can use only the English text will also find valuable and reliable aid in the Lindsay, *The Acts of the Apostles;* Sitterly, *Jerusalem To Rome;* and Scroggie, *The Acts of the Apostles.* Bartlett's contribution on Acts to the *Century Bible,* and that by Blunt in the *Clarendon Bible* are works of reliable scholarship.

As to the General Epistles, Ropes on "St. James" in the *International Critical Commentary* is among the best, based of course on the Greek text. Carr in the *Cambridge Greek Testament* has contributed a helpful volume on "St. James." The English student will find both delight and profit in A. T. Robertson's monograph under the title, *Practical and Social Aspects of Chris-*

tianity, an exposition of James. For the student of the English New Testament one of the best commentaries on James is Plumptre in the *Cambridge Bible.* It is a small, handy, but comprehensive and scholarly work. We would designate as the standard commentary on the epistles of Peter and Jude that by Bigg in the *International Critical Commentary.* In the *Expositor's Greek Testament* Oesterly on James, Hart on I Peter, Strachan on II Peter, and Mayor on Jude are among the best critical works the student can consult. Moffatt's commentary on *The General Epistles* employs his own translation of the New Testament, and is a highly valuable work. Nowhere is the historical and linguistic light better used to illuminate the epistles of James, Peter and Jude. In the *Expositor's Bible* Plummer on James and Jude, and Lumby on the Epistles of Peter are worthy of frequent consultation.

The *Westminister New Testament* has been for many years this interpreter's close companion, and in keeping with that policy he has made large use of Mitchell on "Hebrews and the General Epistles." Linguistically and historically it is a reliable and illuminating interpretation, thoroughly critical though based upon the English text.

We must still give first place among the commentaries on Hebrews to Westcott, though A. B. Bruce must be placed as a very close second. In fact, we hesitate to pronounce Westcott or anyone else superior to Bruce, though the former may have a shade of advantage as a critical commentary. Moffat in the *International Critical Commentary* and Dods in the *Expositor's Greek Testament* are among the best. This writer has referred much and with great profit to Goodspeed on "Hebrews" in the *Bible For Home and School*. The student is referred to Goodspeed's work for a much more thorough bibliography on Hebrews than this brief summary affords. For a rigidly critical study of the book, with special reference to its historical and doctrinal problems, one would do well to use E. F. Scott, *The Epistle To the Hebrews: Its Doctrine and Significance*. Delitsch is old, but still well worth consulting. His intricate knowledge of Old Testament teaching and understanding of the Jewish mind give his book a distinctiveness which will save it from becoming obsolete. Farrar in the *Cambridge Bible* is among the best.

For a review of the historical background of the entire period the student may consult Johannes Weiss, *History of Primitive Christianity*.

This sketch of the literature related to the interpretation of Jewish Christianiy and its products is but a bare suggestion, but from it any student may secure an introduction to the field which can be followed as extensively and minutely as he may wish. We have sought to indicate works which are reliable and adequate for ordinary purposes. The specialist is not here contemplated.

TOPICAL INDEX

Aaron and Christ, 228
Administration in the Jerusalem church, 42
Ananias and Sapphira, 54
Angelology in Judaism, 212
Antioch, evangelization of, 86
Barnabas, 52, 88
Breach between Christianity and Judaism, 197
Community life in the Galilean churches, 30
Community of goods in the Jerusalem church, 50
Cornelius, 83
Deacons, 44
Dispersion of Jerusalem disciples, 39
Destitution, causes of, 57
Dispersion and Christianity 126
Documentary sources of Jewish Christianity, 13
Dorcas, 82
Dynamic of early Christianity, 59
Early Christian life, development of, 20
Early Judaean churches, evidences for, 36
Economic stress, causes of, 57
Elders, 47
Ethiopian eunuch, 79
Evidences for Galatian churches, 27
Faith, heroes of, 260
Fortitude, Christian, 262
Galatian churches, life in, 29
Galatian disciples, 27
Gentile Christianity, 23
Gentile character of primitve Christianity, 200
Gnosticism, 158

Hebrews, interpretation of, 208
Hebrews, introduction to 201
Hebrews, outline, 206
Herodian persecution, 73
Holiness, 264
Holy Spirit, 59
Humanity of Christ, 218
James, 48
James, epistle, interpretation of 106
   introduction, 101
   outline, 105
   martyrdom of 73
   sermon and encyclical, 92
Jerusalem, evangelization of, 76
Jesus, ministry of 20
Jewish Christianity and the Temple, 18
Jewish national hopes, 199
Jewish racial prejudice, 199
Jewish religious sensibilities, 198
Judaism and Christianity, 197
Judaizers, 273
Jude, epistle, interpretation of, 181
   introduction, 177
   outline, 180
Judea, evangelization of, 79
Judean disciples, 36
Levitical priesthood and Christ, 246
Life in early churches, community, 30
   personal, 33
Life in Galatian churches, 29
Life in the Jerusalem church, 37
Literature on Jewish Christianity, 279
Martyrdom of Stephen, 69

dek, 233, 242
of Palestinian
 ıity, 58
 of administration
Jerusalem Christi-
y, 42
ıd Christ compared

ion, Herodian, 73
ion, Pharisaic, 68
ion, Sadducean, 64
 life in early
ches, 33
rst epistle, inter-
 ation, 135
 ıduction, 129
 ne, 133
 ısoned, 74
 ionary activities, 81
nd epistle, inter-
 ation, 164
 ıduction, 157
 ne, 163
ıon in the house of
ıelius, 92
'entecost, 90
re the Sanhedrin,

Peter, sermon in the Temple, 91
Pharisaic persecution, 68
Phases of development in early Christian life, 20
Philip and the eunuch, 79
Priesthood of Christ, 228
Prophetic revelation, 210
Reactionary Jewish Christianity, 273
Rest, the eternal, 225
Sadducean persecution, 64
Samaria, evangelization of, 174
Second coming of Christ, 174
Simon the tanner, 85
Sources, documentary, 13
Stephen martyrdom of, 69
Stephen's sermon, 91
Synagogue, influence on Christianity, 95
Tabernacle service, 252
Temporal support in the Jerusalem church, 50.
Temple, 18

SCRIPTURE INDEX

ACTS
1:1-14	59
1:15-26	42
2:1-13	59
2:14-40	90
2:5-42	64
2:43-47	52
3:1-26	65
3:12-26	91
4:1-22	66
4:8-12	91
4:23-31	59
4:32-5:11	50
4:31-37	64
5:12-42	68
6:1-6	42
6:7	76
6:8-15	69
7:1-53	91
8:1-3	72
8:4-40	76
9:11-11:26	76
10:34-43	92
11:27-30	46
12:1-23	73
12:34	76
15:1-29	42
15:13-21	92

JAMES
1:1	106
1:2-8	107
1:9-11	109
1:12-18	110
1:19-27	111
2:1-13	112
2:14-26	113
3:1-12	115
3:13-18	117
4:1-10	119
4:11-5:6	120
5:7-11	122
5:12-18	123
5:19-20	125

I PETER
1:1, 2	135
1:3-12	137
1:13-25	139
2:1-10	143
2:11-17	145
2:18-25	147
3:1-6	148
3:7	149
3:8-12	150
3:13-17	151
3:18-21	152
4:1-11	153
4:12-19	154
5:1-11	156
5:12-14	157

II PETER
1:1, 2	164
1:3-11	165
1:12-21	167
2:1-9	169
2:10-22	172
3:1-7	174
3:8-13	175
3:14-18	176

JUDE
1, 2	181
3, 4	182
5-7	183
8-11	186
12-16	188
17-19	191
20-23	193
24, 25	194

HEBREWS
1:1-3	210
1:4-14	212
2:1-4	215
2:5-18	217
3:1, 2	220
3:3-6	221
3:7-14	222
3:15-4:2	223
4:3-13	225
4:14-5:3	228
5:4-6	232
5:7-10	233
5:11-6:3	234
6:4-6	239
6:7, 8	240
6:9-20	241
7:1-3	243
7:4-10	244
7:11-19	247
7:20, 21	247
7:23-25	248
7:26-8:5	248
8:6-13	250
9:1-22	252
9:23-28	255
10:1-4	256
10:5-18	257
10:19-25	258
10:26-31	259
10:32-38	259
10:39	260
11:1-12	261
11:13-40	262
12:1	262
12:2-13	263
12:14-17	264
12:18-29	265
13:1-7	267
13:8-17	268
13:18-25	268

www.ingramcontent.com/pod-product-compliance
Lightning Source LLC
Chambersburg PA
CBHW050340230426
43663CB00010B/1927